Belgium, a State of Mind

Belgium, *a State of Mind*

Text
Olivier Mouton
Marie-Anne Wilssens
Frédéric Antoine
Marc Reynebeau

Photografie
Jean-Claude Samoy

lannoo | *Racine*

This book is also available in Dutch (Uitgeverij Lannoo), French (Editions Racine) and German (Grenz Echo Verlag).

This publication marks the occasion of the Belgian Chairmanship of the Council of the European Union (1 July – 31 December 2001) in collaboration with the Prime Minister's Office, the Office of the Minister of Foreign Affairs, and the Ministry of Foreign Affairs, Trade and Development Aid.

The following contributed to the book:

Authors
Olivier Mouton
Marie-Anne Wilssens
Frédéric Antoine
Marc Reynebeau

Contributors
Insets: Famous and Memorable Belgians: Lieve Reynebeau (except for "Marguerite Yourcenar" by Michèle Goslar)

Vignettes: Yves Desmet, Catherine Vuylsteke, Michael Stabenow, Marijke Libert, Isabelle Lemal, Luc Van der Kelen, Anna Luyten, Gabriëlle Lefèvre, Miel Dekeyser, Isabelle Philippon, Dominike Van Besien, Hugues Dayez, Leo Bonte, Guy Lemaire, Christian Laporte, Veerle Windels.

Photography
Jean-Claude Samoy

Iconography
see photo captions

English translation
Frank Parker (Ch. 1); Alastair Weir (Ch.2) and Valerie Caroll (Ch.3)
Insets and vignettes by Alastair Weir and Valerie Caroll

Graphic Design
communicationmatters, Antwerp
paperback cover by Keppens' Kreaties, Ghent

© Uitgeverij Lannoo, Tielt and the Belgian Ministry of Foreign Affairs – 2001
ISBN 90 209 4464 9 (Lannoo)
ISBN 2-87386-256-4 (Racine)
NUGI 672 - SBO 35
Registration : 2002/45/374 (Lannoo) - D.2001, 6852.08 (Racine)
2nd printrun
Printed and bound by Drukkerij Lannoo nv, Tielt - 2001

www.lannoo.com

Foreword

A Belgian is by nature disinclined to set himself up as the centre of attention. 'What is the point?', you hear him say. Fortunately some of them do have a habit of talking nineteen to the dozen about the country and its inhabitants. So for this book we called on a clutch of authors, each of whom offer their own view on this complicated bit of Europe. In Belgium we do not all need to be on the same wavelength. Our diversity is our greatest strength, our creativity our most important commodity, our non-conformity our greatest virtue.

Although these same Belgian authors may be happy to run themselves down and self-mockery is never far off, it is plain from their articles how proud they are of their country and how difficult they find it to feel at home anywhere else. In many respects the Belgian is his own severest critic, yet one with a charitable view of his fellow citizens, and when it comes to government, both attitudes apply. He never thinks any government is good enough, can always tell you what should be improved and how, and says so in words and print often quite mercilessly, well knowing that people swapping words don't make war. Because after all, we live in a free country, they say, and free men can speak their mind.

Belgium is a surprising country, with as many contradictions and as many opportunities for compromise and cooperation as there are Belgians. Belgium is one of those countries where the urge for social organization is most highly developed. When three Belgians come together, they form a league, a club, a party or an association of some sort. A fourth Belgian makes himself into a link, to collect together groups from the same nest or with the same convictions. All these groups together make up the real country, which every citizen, every government and certainly every legislator has to take into consideration.

In the country of Reynard the Fox and Till Eulenspiegel one is never far from mild irony. Yet life is good here. And, as well as Poirot and Tin Tin, this small area has produced a whole series of other well-known characters. It's just that no one realizes that Jacques Brel and Gerard Mortier are Belgians. So it is time to turn the floodlights on our country, and the presidency of the European Union is a good excuse to do so. We take this opportunity to show you that Belgium is more than just the place where most of the European institutions are established, and hope you will enjoy discovering the things that can make a little country a great one.

Guy Verhofstadt
Prime Minister

Louis Michel
Deputy Prime Minister and
Minister of Foreign Affairs

Summary

Chapter 3   Frédéric Antoine
Famous and Memorable Belgians – They, too, are Belgians

Marc Reynebeau

Introducing Belgium

The Country as a Mirror of its People

Olivier Mouton

As a title for a painting depicting the land of his birth, the surrealist painter René Magritte might well have chosen "Ceci n'est pas la Belgique." (This is not Belgium.). "Billions of blue blistering barnacles" would undoubtedly have been the reaction of Tintin's Captain Haddock, had he been asked to explain the complex situation of his country to journalists attending a European summit in Brussels. For his part, film director André Delvaux would have opted for a hazy landscape with trains criss-crossing before the fleeting shadow of a palely beautiful, but mysterious Miss Belgium. The spectator himself is left to his own devices in discovering the soul of a country. And this without succumbing to the uproar so well described by Hugo Claus, the Flemish author who figures each year on the list of favourites for the Nobel Prize for Literature.

It is no accident that this small country at the heart of the European Union proved to be the ideal breeding ground for Surrealism, comic strips and magic realism films. The fact that it is a buffer state between two big European powers, Germany and France, a border state between the two big cultural basins of the Union, a complex state, with three language communities, has not prevented Belgium from developing its own identity during 170 years of existence, an

This world-famous painting by the Belgian surrealist René Magritte (1898-1967) plays on the discrepancy between the portrayal and the subject portrayed. The need to put things into perspective apparent in the words *Ceci n'est pas une pipe* (This is not a pipe) is a perfect illustration of the character of the Belgians.
© Sabam

This detail of a Peasant Wedding, painted by Pieter Breughel the Elder (1525/30-1569), shows the passion of the Belgians' ancestors for the art of dining and the noble grape.
© Kunsthistorisches Museum, Vienna

identity uncertain, but firm, fragile but ambitious. An identity, moreover, that is sometimes difficult to grasp, that perhaps may well be the "being Belgian" so dear to Jacques Brel, a mixture of unrestrained joy and deep melancholy, of unbounded hope and an almost morbidly critical mind.

The Belgian is both a pragmatist and an Epicurean, and knows the tricks of pulling strings to make life as agreeable as possible. Deep within himself, however, he conserves a healthy measure of self-mockery. As a figure from local folklore, he would be a cross between Till Eulenspiegel, Charles de Coster's brave hero, and Manneken Pis, the waggish statue just a stone's throw from the Brussels Grand Place. Not forgetting, of course, Tchantchè, the symbol of Liège, because the Belgian knows how to enjoy life's pleasures to the full. A single painting of Breughel the Elder says it all: few countries cultivate with such passion the art of nobly wining and dining. And to give greater emphasis to their life style, Bruxellois, Flemings and Walloons join their voices in singing a hymn of resourcefulness and ingenuity, accompanied from the four corners of the world by the classic tones of Helmut Lotti or the modern beat of the group Deus. They are unceasing in their discovery of new formulas to perpetuate their own welfare.

The surrealist soul of the Belgians surfaces even when flying kites on the beach. This strange kite, shaped like two legs whirling through the sky, may illustrate this.

When it comes to securing his own personal comfort, indeed, the Belgian will do exactly as he pleases. At the same time, he is prepared to listen to others and to accept their otherness. Belgium is a hospitable country and it is therefore no accident that it is constantly evolving, transforming itself and daily rediscovering itself. Belgium is also a multicultural country, a laboratory for the Europe that is under construction. On its small 30,500 square kilometres of territory, 10 million citizens are busy giving joint and unequivocal form to their existence.

A Federal State, Constantly Rethinking Itself

Anyone recounting the saga of the land of the Belgians would lard his story with numerous anecdotes and conflicts. It is true, there is sometimes quite a bit of rumbling between the country's two communities: 5.9 million Flemings and 3.3 million Walloons, not to mention the 1 million Bruxellois. In the same way as Asterix's village, obstinately continuing to offer resistance, certain places draw a great deal of attention, particularly along the line of the language border that was fixed definitively in 1963. These are often small, picturesque villages where the languages meet, sometimes leading to confrontation. It can also happen that one of those villages becomes an obsession, causing government no end of headache. In the past, this sort of problem proved to be a stumbling block for some administrations, though no longer. Journalists from all over the world have often seized on such small incidents to diagnose the malaise of this small, unknown country and even to caricature it. The language problem may be a fact of life, but it does not dominate the political landscape.

Indeed, one has only to stand back a little to see that the actuality is different from what the endemic conflicts suggest. In spite of its numerous socio-economic realities and divergent identities, Belgium has always been able to adapt. "Non-violence and common sense", as put by André Miroir, Professor at the Université libre de Bruxelles and co-author of a recent work on conflicts between the communities in Belgium. Without consciously meaning to, the country has even given form to a model for the peaceful solution of conflicts, one of the major charac-

teristics of which is the famous *compromis à la belge*, the Belgian compromise. Moving from reform to reform, institutions have adapted themselves to provide as faithful as possible a reflection of the diversity of the population. Today, Brussels, the capital, is a bilingual region that certain people would like to hold up as an example of a solution for the thorny question of the status of Jerusalem. Various delegations have examined the country's amazing tangle of councils and governments, whose strength is that they work. Just one further instance of this is provided by the German community, 70,000 strong, the most protected minority in the world.

The history of this constitutional monarchy, whose present sovereign is Albert II, begins offici-ally in 1830 with the country's independence, though several historians place the start a few decades earlier and some even a couple of centuries earlier. Xavier Mabille, author of the refe-rence work *Histoire politique de la Belgique*, puts it around 1780. In his view, the period from

14

For careerists in national politics, membership in the Christian-Democratic party was until recently an all-risks insurance policy against a period in opposition. If in addition you lived in Flanders, the most densely populated region of the country, then you had all the trumps in your hand to gain the leadership of the federal government. Apart from a short interruption in the early 1950s, this had always been the case since the Second World War. However, in the late summer of 1999 things changed. For the first time in the history of this country, a rainbow government emerged: a coalition of Socialists, Liberals and Greens. Until then it was the Flemish Christian-Democrats in particular who had supplied Prime Ministers and shaped the political landscape. Breaking this link has not, however, drastically changed the profile of the Belgian politician. He is usually perceived as a mischievous personality, preferably a fervent football fan, who frequently appears in the stands among the most exuberant supporters, and who, in contrast to the good and the great who are convinced of their own omnipotence, is not at all condescending. He is by nature more modest and appears to adapt himself to the restricted dimensions of the territory over which he exercises his petty authority. Unquestionably he is more aware of the limited scope for his activities, as he is of the fact that in the last 30 years his profession has lost much of its prestige because the

number of its representatives has multiplied. Through the successive reforms of the constitution, which have weakened federal powers ever further to the advantage of the country's regions and communities, the number of titled posts in Belgium has grown enormously. Considering the number of inhabitants, Belgium is one of the countries with the largest number of ministers.

Most Belgians are baffled by the complicated structure of their country: they are lost in the labyrinth of institutions. Abroad, however, the structure has won much admiration. The foreign specialists who come here to study the delicate institutional clockwork, with the object of learning something from it for their own use, are legion. This little country, on the border between the Latin and Germanic cultures, divided into three regions, three communities and ten provinces, has always proved able to keep its communal demons under control, by means of wise arbitration, nightly palavers, and consensual decisions which could only happen in the country of the surrealist Magritte. The Belgian politician is continually balancing on a slack rope. He has to perform formidable feats to keep all the federal entities satisfied. The smallest psychological error can make the communal flames flare up again, and cause the umpteenth government to stumble on the institutional battlefield. In the heat of the strife he often has to negotiate like a marriage counsellor to prevent a total break between the two most important communities of the realm. Some have compared him to a plumber who, monkey-wrench within reach, must continually tighten up the loosened bolts of the Belgian institutional meccano. Tightrope walker, trick-cyclist or institutional plumber, the Belgian politician must in any case excel in the art of compromise. If he wants to survive he must more than ever have the art of balancing between North and South at his fingertips. This used to be called waffle-iron politics, in which a section of Walloon motorway was authorised as a counterweight to Flemish harbour works. Certainly now he must work in the bosom of a rainbow coalition of six parties, and quartered between the authoritarian line of certain liberal authorities, the laissez-faire attitude of the Greens, and the sometimes irreconcilable Flemish and French-speaking mentalities, the Belgian federal politician with responsibility often has

the greatest difficulty in finding a common denominator acceptable to everyone in this small world. His consensual decisions are therefore often so sophisticated and inconsistent in the most dangerous passages that neither ordinary citizens nor constitutional lawyers are capable of getting to the bottom of all their contradictions. But meanwhile the consensus remains a fact, and the stumbling block has been overcome. That is truly the most remarkable quality of the Belgian politician: despite his modesty, with a typical Belgian preference for pragmatism, he is capable of clearing the mines from the most prickly political situations.

Isabelle Philippon

Journalist with the weekly Le Vif - L'Express

1780 to 1830 represented a transitional period between the end of the Ancien Regime and the foundation of an independent, constitutional state. The sum and substance of Belgium were already present in latent form and their development was gradual. The Belgian constitution is one of the most liberal in the world and right from the start it recognised the freedom of the individual, of religion, of education, of the press, of association and of assembly, and not least of language. In spite of this, the French bourgeoisie were to dominate unitary Belgium for nearly a century, equilibrium being restored only during the first half of the 20th century by way of Flemish emancipation. However, the call for reform is never far away and Professor Calculus is there, preparing his magic, institutional formulas.

The first real reform of the state took place in 1970, a few years after the "Leuven Affair", when the French-speakers were constrained to quit the university town and build Louvain-La-Neuve, another symbol in the history of the Communities. Time and again, original models for living together have been worked out. The reform of 1970 laid the foundations for a federal Belgian state and for an institutional landscape worthy of the futuristic and imaginary creations of the artist François Schuiten, author of *Cités obscures* (Dark Cities), one of which is Brüsel.

Manneken Pis is not far from the Grand Place in Brussels. This small statue, after a seventeenth-century model of a little boy piddling, is a tourist attraction. From the Middle Ages to today, Belgian art has alluded to man's primal needs without any diffidence.

Two strands of logic intertwine. The one is economic and territorial, and has led to the establishment of three regions: Brussels, Flanders and Wallonia. The other is cultural and linguistic, which at the same time has resulted in the creation of three communities: the Flemish, the French and the German. What follows could be a lesson in Post-modern logic. The Flemish Community consists of Flanders and the Dutch-speaking population of Brussels; for the sake of simplicity, however, the Flemings decided at the outset to merge their regional and community institutions. The French Community consists of Wallonia and the French-speaking population of Brussels, but, in this case, the institutions have not been merged. The German Community, lastly, is simply a small part of the Walloon Region that borders on Germany and is inhabited by about 70,000 speakers of German, who are among the most fervent defenders of Belgium.

Brussels became a fully fledged, bilingual region in 1989 and has its own institutions. With one million inhabitants, the city functions as a laboratory of cohabitation and forms a permanent meeting place of the various communities. It is also the capital of Europe, of federal Belgium, of Flanders and of the French Community. To get this model to work, all the ingenuity of the Belgian legislator had to be called upon. Four governments and four assemblies administer the various affairs of region and community. And then, of course, there are the 19 municipalities of this tiny territory.

Masters Of Democracy

Phew! There you have them. The broad outlines of the Belgian state as it is at present – no simple matter. Since 1970, various other state reforms on the basis of these principles have given an entirely new look to the country. Even the former Prime Minister Gaston Eyskens declared, "The old paternalistic Belgium is dead." The time has come when each community and each region can work out a policy properly adapted to its own specific needs. The extremely democratic principle on which this development rests has the barbaric name of "subsidiarity": in other words, the managing of matters as close to the level of the citizen as possible, not that he will be any the wiser. The complex edifice that is Belgium sometimes sins in lacking transparency, as exemplified by the fact that certain competences are in the hands of six or seven different ministers, which necessarily requires consultation at all times between the various levels of power. This federal puzzle is nevertheless a true reflection of the people. Surrealist, one might say; creative, too; sometimes roguish; always pragmatic; ingenious when it comes to developing societal models.

In the constant process of adjustment, Belgium plays the democracy card, though it goes without saying that the requisite political agreements have been brokered in plush salons worthy of the Chateau of Marlinspike – Homeric discussions behind closed doors of buildings with such romantic-sounding names as Stuyvenberg, Lambermont or Hertoginnedal. Never satisfied, the Belgian would have liked to keep an attentive eye on proceedings, say his piece and add a few of his chosen formulas. Sooner or later, though, he will have his say, as he is obliged to vote at six or seven levels of government, depending on where he lives: municipality, province, regional or community assembly, Chamber of Representatives and Senate, and European

Albert II became king of the Belgians in 1993 on the sudden death of his brother Baudouin. Just as Baudouin at the end of his days showed himself as a ruler who opposed the traffic in women, so Albert II sets himself up as the defender of the rights of children.
© Van Parys Media

The Atomium is the most celebrated relic of the 1958 world exhibition. This structure by André Waterkeyn, a chartered engineer, is composed of nine spheres representing the structure of an iron crystalline molecule then recently discovered by science. Each sphere represents one atom, enlarged 165 billion times.
© ATOMIUM – Sominex autorisation n° 21-417

Parliament. And he knows how best to use his democratic power, regularly taking the opportunity of indicating his dissatisfaction with one or other party or of giving smaller parties a little more muscle.

The political landscape of Belgium bears no resemblance at all to the *mer du Nord pour dernier terrain vague* (the North Sea as the final wasteland) that Jacques Brel sang about. On the contrary, it is now a question of a complex society and a complex edifice. With the Belgian electoral system being one of proportional representation, parliamentary seats are spread among numerous political formations. At the latest parliamentary elections, held in June 1999, no less than six parties in Flanders gained seats in the assembly. A coalition of four was needed for a majority to be formed at regional level: the VLD (Liberals), the SP (Socialists), Agalev (Greens), and VU-ID (Flemish Nationalists). In Wallonia, "just" four parties gained representation, three of which formed a governing coalition: PRL-FDF-MCC (Liberals, affiliated to a democratic front of French-speaking Bruxellois and a Christian-Democrat breakaway group), PS (Socialists) and Ecolo (Greens). For the first time in 40 years, the Christian-Democrat parties (CVP and PSC)

Design for a balloon on the occasion
of the Belgian Presidency of the
Council of the European Union

20

Three communities, three regions, two languages, half of the country tied closely to a Germanic culture, the other half to a Romance one. All the ingredients are there to make Belgium the Balkans on the North Sea, and yet it remains remarkably peaceful, apart from the occasional firecracker and a few hotheads drenched by water cannon. Belgium is not a country of great political emotions, and even less of utopias. The Belgians do not believe in the possibility of a society being made perfect and know that that can only result in chaos, civil war and dictatorship.

The greatest democratic strength of the Belgians is their innate aversion to and distrust of any form of government authority. A legacy, it is said, of the historical fate to have been one of the most occupied nations of Europe. The Belgian accepts authority, but prefers to arrange his affairs on the side, in the often grey area between the law and illegality. Stubborn, and without shouting it from the rooftops, this is a nation of resistance fighters, sober anarchists who nod politely to every policeman and then hurry home to quickly circumvent the tax laws. The Belgian attitude to the great ideologies has been best expressed by Gaston Eyskens, a legendary prime minister. He said, "Principles are like wind. You hold on as long as you can, and then, as quietly as possible, let go." Pragmatism, solving problems, fixing things,

keeping things under control, and the internal arrangement of differences of opinion, are part of the national character of the Belgian people and their leaders. In Belgian politics the drivel flows in streams; blood rarely, if ever.

Belgian politics are a palaver in true African style. Should we do it this way? No? Then let's try that way, or even better, here's another way out. And then we start all over again. This is how we have meanwhile reached our 10th definitive reform of the constitution, which again is already out of date. Always after years of preparation in discussion groups, sealed with lengthy conclaves at which the log jams are broken. Slowly, frustratingly slowly, as befits a democracy. But with the enormous advantage that this incredibly complex country, with its countless, nonetheless insoluble contrasts and conflicts of interest, still always comes out surviving without a drop of blood being spilt.

Belgians are law-abiding anarchists, who channel their opposition into fooling the government and in eternal grumbling. Belgium is, in short, a model democracy.

Yves Desmet
Chief political editor, daily De Morgen.

The eighteenth-century Palais des Nations (1778-1783) by the architect Barnabé Guimard is a model of brilliant neoclassicism. This is the home of the Belgian parliament, where the Chamber of Deputies and Senate carry out their legislative duties.
© Oswald Pauwels

found themselves everywhere except in Brussels on the opposition benches, facing a "rainbow" coalition led by the Liberal Prime Minister Guy Verhofstadt.

This is yet another area where Belgium casts around for formulas to keep up with the times. A parliamentary commission is studying new ways of conducting the democratic process, including the referendum; some people, indeed, would like to see the proportional electoral system combined with a majority system, in order to achieve greater clarity in the political landscape. Searching, searching, ever searching. George Simenon, the renowned author of detective novels, including the Maigret series, would certainly have felt at home in this perpetual questing for signs of democracy.

The Belgians are masters at democracy, that much is certain. And not just where the ballot box

and institutions are concerned. The discovery in 1996 of the bodies of those girls murdered in such gruesome circumstances by the criminal Marc Dutroux, whose name is now known all round the world, brought a good 300,000 people onto the streets to voice their indignation. This protest, which has gone into the history books as The White March, forced the political world to institute an urgent reform of the justice system and the police, reform that 2001 and 2002 will see in full swing. Reform, as if one's life depended on it. Adapt. Change. Belgium stood at the edge of the abyss and stepped back from it. Didier Pavy, Brussels correspondent of the Nouvel Observateur, saw the march and all those that followed it as "a sign of a recovery", "a desire to rehabilitate the citizen".

Just as elsewhere in Europe, the spirit of democracy is sometimes darkened in Belgium. A worrying development is the strong showing of the Far Right in Flanders, where the Vlaams Blok (the xenophobic and independence party of the Far Right) has picked up 15 per cent of the votes. To prevent it gaining power, particularly in Antwerp, where it received 33 per cent of the votes in the local elections in October, a democratic cordon sanitaire has been thrown around it. Ways and means are constantly being sought to diminish, to eradicate the problem. Artists like the writer Tom Lanoye, moreover, are using their imagination to help democracy triumph. Indeed, we see here a paradoxical expression of a country that has never been used to regarding itself critically or to be withdrawn into itself. Quite the contrary.

Prince Philip inherited the leadership of the Belgian trade missions abroad from his father. Blue blood is still sometimes useful for opening doors, to the bene-fit of Belgian business. His visit to Thailand in February 2001 had the object of strengthening trade relations between the two countries. Such visits are also combined with a little sight-seeing. © Reuters

24

Exporting: An Unceasing Drive!

The smaller a country is, the more open it is to the outside world. That is simply force of circumstances. In Belgium, looking beyond the horizon has become an art, a way of life. From the moment of its creation, the country developed a lively and innovative economy, international in its approach. Again, it is no accident that Belgium was one of the major driving forces behind the Industrial Revolution of the 19th century, when it captured a leading position on world markets. Between the time of independence in 1830 and the end of that century, Belgium's textile industry expanded by 800 per cent, the Verviers woollen industry by 700 per cent, the coal-mining industry by 800 per cent and the foundry industry by 1,400 per cent. This development was accompanied by the inevitable social conflicts, as portrayed in Stijn Coninx's film *Daens*, though this was perhaps the price that had to be paid for prosperity.

And there were flagship companies in those days, too. One example was Solvay, in the field of chemistry, which set up subsidiaries throughout Europe and even in Russia. Another was Empain, in the field of electrical engineering, which built the Paris Metro and laid tram-tracks in China and Egypt. This brief review of the country's golden age also has to include the lightning-fast development of the metallurgy and coal-mining industries. Belgium's visiting card abroad – the Generale Maaatschappij – had a presence in Russia, China and Mexico. Between, 1908 and 1961, the Congo, the giant of Central Africa, was under little Belgium's tutelage. It was no doubt a sign of the times that the ceding in 1988 of the majority of the Generale

Mathilde d'Udeken d'Acoz's attractive smile increased the popularity of the Belgian royal family among the population. Prince Philip's marriage to this noble lady led to a very typical chocolate box romanticism.

Maatschappij's shares was the subject of an unprecedented media-cum-financial saga. Today, the French Suez Group still holds a two-thirds participation, though this has not prevented federal Belgium from continuing to place its stamp on the company.

In adapting, Belgium has been helped by economic development. The tertiary sector has expanded and the new economy has blossomed in this small territory, which, by the way, has the densest network of cables in the world. Little by little, the big industries are moving out and giving way to a whole raft of new initiatives. It is a development that got under way earlier in Flanders than in Wallonia, where government aid was sometimes used to keep certain enterprises afloat. In the meantime, the southern part of the country has had a salutary awakening and now all three regions are straining every nerve. Employment figures in Belgium speak volumes. Between 1995 and 1999, the number of those working in the secondary sector declined from 936,000 to 909,000; over the same period, the number of those employed in the tertiary sector rose from 2,691 to 2,844. To take just a couple of other significant figures: if the 1995 figure for metalworking production is equal to 100, the 1999 figure equals 101.6, which indicates relative stagnation; however, if the 1985 figure for corporate services is equal to 100, the 1999 figure for them equals 514.1, with a remarkable acceleration of growth during the final five years.

Right from the outset, one feature that has characterised the economy of Belgium more than this astounding capacity to adapt has been the urge to export. Globalization – the word that is in everyone's mouth these days – has long been an established fact of life for the country. Thanks to the efforts of companies that have followed Tintin and Bobby to the four corners of the world, consumers everywhere are able to locate little Belgium on the map. Supported in their endeavours by Prince Philip and Princess Mathilde, these companies are, moreover, contributing to the prosperity and image of the country. A few more figures? In 1999, Belgium, representing 0.2 per cent of the world's population, accounted for 3.3 per cent of world exports. Within the European Union, Belgium's share of the population is just 2.9 per cent, but it generates 8 per cent of the exports. The ratio of Belgium's exports to Gross Domestic Product (GDP), lastly, is a significant 70.9 per cent.

The list of this tiny country's merits continues: number one in the world for the export of diamonds and carpets, number two for the export of vegetable fibres, chocolate and margarine, number three for glass, number four for eggs, non-alcoholic drinks and vehicles, number five for sugar and photographic products, etc. Running down the list of companies that gained the Royal Export Award last year, one comes across a host of symbols of Belgium, including Chimay beers, barriers from Automatic Systems and communications systems from Telindus. The Belgian leitmotif of adaptation and change runs through this domain as it does through others. External trade has recently been regionalised, meaning that each region is now contributing autonomously to the economic sparkle of the country. With their activities co-ordinated by a federal agency headed by Prince Philip, the heir to the throne, a new and bountiful era has dawned.

A True Multicultural Tradition

The economic dynamism exhibited by Belgium has made the country a meeting place in all senses of the word. Workers from all around the world have arrived here to contribute to the country's growth, so much so that Belgium can boast a true multicultural tradition. The country of gourmets is consequently able to savour dishes from everywhere in the world, served up in restaurants with exotic-sounding names. Troupes bursting with talent play on the boards of the theatres; sensual flamenco regularly fires Scandinavian frescoes, sometimes marked by an African narrative. A heady cocktail! And then there are the football fields, whose grasses exhibit a cosmopolitan array of legs chasing the ball.

What few people know is that the first great migration from Belgium was in fact to Belgium. During the 19th century, Flanders was faced with serious economic difficulties, whereas Wallonia had claimed a place as an industrial world power. In his book, *In de Rue des Flamands*, journalist and author Guido Fonteyn writes, "To escape their misery, hundreds of thousands of

For centuries Belgium has been a crossroads where different cultures meet, with splendid cultural tours de force emerging from these melting pots. Abdelaziz Sanokh's Ghent dance company Hush Hush Hush is an assemblage of many nationalities and presents innovative choreographic creations with an international reputation. A scene from the production of 2Pack.
© Wim Van Capellen

Flemings left their native soil in search of work, more particularly in Wallonia." Despite initial mistrust, based on racial clichés, it was a fruitful intermingling. Indeed, many of the current crop of politicians from Wallonia – Onckelinx, Van Cauwenberghe, Reynders and others – trace their roots to that movement. Belgium, with her two major cultural and linguistic communities, is thus quite clearly an ideal cradle for the mingling of various peoples.

The next wave of migration got under way at the beginning of the 20th century and reached a peak just after the Second World War. The revival of industries devastated by war demanded a great deal of labour. The mines in particular suffered from a shortage and production had fallen from 4.4 million tonnes in 1939 to 2.2 million during the Occupation. The Coal-mining Federation began a massive roundup of workers, chiefly in the villages of Italy, and a protocol was signed permitting 77,000 Italians to come and work in Belgium, principally in Hainault and to a lesser extent in Limburg. Integration was not always smooth, but many Italians now regard Belgium as their second fatherland. Italian restaurants, groceries and other shops are legion. Certain Italians have gained themselves an enviable place, such as the singer Adamo or the footballer Enzo Scifo. The massive influx of Italians enabled the "battle for coal" to be won and by 1953 production had risen to 5 million tonnes. However, an end to this particular great phase of migration was signalled by the trauma of the mine disaster at Bois-du-Cazier on 8 August 1956, in which 262 people, many of them Italians, lost their lives in a gas explosion. The drama served to root the Italian community even deeper within Belgium and each year there is a remembrance ceremony. Belgium, a land of hospitality.

Other countries were subsequently tapped for workers, including Spain, Portugal, Greece and Morocco. During the mid-1960s, there was a substantial flow of Turks into the country. When the oil crises of the 1970s struck, however, the brake was applied and the borders were closed, now being open only for the purposes of reuniting families. The manner of receiving foreigners into

The crooner Adamo is an Italian immigrant. Like many of his compatriots he regards Belgium as his home. This Sicilian Belgian is regarded as one of their most highly valued fellow citizens by the Belgians.
AMSAB/Sabena

Introducing Belgium. The Country as a Mirror of its People

the country remains a particularly sensitive, political question. Confronted with a growing flood of asylum applications, as well as to prevent the organisation of networks for the trafficking of human beings, the government has recently amended its asylum policy, so that, instead of receiving financial support from public social welfare centres, asylum seekers now receive material help. It is a policy that reflects the general line of thought within the European Union.

The intermingling of races is nevertheless a fact. Today, one in ten Belgians has foreign antecedents. As of 1 January 1999, indeed, 891,980 inhabitants of Belgium were of foreign extraction, a good 8.7 per cent of the overall population. And while, for historical reasons, Hainault remains an open province, Brussels, the capital of the European Union, is undoubtedly the multicultural city of tomorrow: 272,146 of its inhabitants are of foreign extraction, i.e. 28.5 per cent of the overall population of the region, though the European institutions naturally have much to do with this new destiny. Brussels – capital of Belgium, but also the seat of the Commission, of the Council of the European Union and of the European Parliament – together with Strasbourg – the seat of the Committee of the Regions, of the Economic and Social Committee and of the West-European Union – has thrown its arms open to the thousands of officials from the 15 (soon to be the 25 or 30) member states of the Union. NATO, likewise with its headquarters in Brussels, provides an additional reinforcement of this cosmopolitan character. All this is tangible, both in the streets and in the culture, which is continually on the lookout for new languages to absorb. Brussels – border town, chief city of the European fatherland – is transmuting its fault lines into lines of force and incorporating its multi-coloured talents, in order to give direction to its future.

Multicultural Belgium. My Guinean friend does not understand what is meant by it, although he had observed that artistic Flemings used these words most often when they were discussing the latest grant application. "Oh that," he ended up saying, and dished up a few reminiscences: such as the incident in a Brussels video shop, when his hard-earned 12 € note was branded as counterfeit and the lady behind the till would only hire anything out "to your sort of people" in return for holding their identity card. Worse still was an earlier attempt to go out dancing in Europe's capital city. Characters with more brawn than brain refused us entry to one establishment after another. Accusations of racism? "Oh, nothing personal, sir, just that you haven't got a membership card." Really?

And yet, my Guinean friend goes on, Belgium is extremely multicultural. Can't you hear almost all the languages of Babel in the Brussels telephone booths with their acoustically virtually non-existent cardboard walls, and don't the many exotic shops and supermarkets flog all imaginable ingredients of the world? He is quite confident: everyone is here, Belgium is just like Noah's Ark. Each to his own, admittedly: the many ethnic groups live alongside each other rather than with each other. But that particular aspect, adds my Chinese friend, in fact applies most to the autochthonous groups of the population. They live in separate worlds, without much interest in, or interference from, each other. When he swapped a French-speaking job in Brussels for one a few miles out of the capital, in Flanders, my Chinese friend felt like a displaced migrant worker for months. Stakhanov, he would sometimes sourly remark later, must surely have been a Fleming, and there is no doubt that the word 'stakhanovism' was thought up by a French speaker. The difference between word and deed.

But does Belgium, which calls itself multicultural, not play the same trick too? What else can you think of the disgrace of the Vlaams Blok? Oh, my former neighbours, who were Turks, have no problems with it in Ghent; they voted for it themselves. You do not understand, they explain, but these hordes of Eastern Europeans – my Guinean friend with his racist inclinations and even less love calls them faux blancs – ruin our lives with their mafias and their black-market competition. Maybe the Vlaams Blok will send them home, don't you think?

Catherine Vuylsteke

Journalist with the daily De Morgen.

31

The mix of many nationalities is a fact: one in ten Belgians is a foreigner.

Belgium performs an important role in Europe. In the European parliament all the flags of the European member states fly proudly beside each other in brotherly harmony. The creativity displayed by the Belgians in their federal model is an ideal source of inspiration for the structure of the European Union.

A Permanent Laboratory For Europe

It could be said that Belgium, in the same way as her capital, acts as a permanent laboratory for Europe. Situated at the heart of the continent, this little country exhibits wonderfully well the characteristics of a union under constant construction. The Belgians are unceasing in adapting their institutions, in creating new forums for dialogue and thereby finding solutions for the inevitable conflicts that arise between various cultures and languages. This already represents a political project in itself. The present generation of politicians has been fired by a number of great statesmen in its quest to achieve a harmonious society in Belgium and to deepen the foundations of Europe, and is unremitting in pursuing this dual aspiration, albeit that some of those politicians see, in an ultimate Europe of regions, a decisive development that would satisfy their thirst for autonomy.

Among the great figures who regarded themselves as Belgian and who became beacons for Europe, three deserve mention here. And, as is only right and proper in this complex country, their choice is a perfectly balanced reflection of the three major political tendencies. The first of them, the Socialist Paul-Henri Spaak, several times Foreign Minister after the Second World War, as well as Prime Minister, was one of the key figures in the reconstruction of Europe. The first chairman of the Consultative Assembly of the Council of Europe, he resigned amidst great clamour because of the failure of federalist plans to make it a legislative council. It was preci-

After the Second World War, the socialist Paul-Henri Spaak was one of the protagonists of the expansion of Europe. 'The future belongs to the great human communities, of that I have no doubt.'
AMSAB/© R. Kayaert

As minister of Foreign Affairs, Pierre Harmel played a leading role in the unification of Europe. He believed that Great Britain had to be included in the then European Economic Community.
AMSAB/© J. De Well

sely his federalist vision that made it possible later for the process of building Europe to be relaunched at Messina in 1955. Spaak, who headed a committee of experts, drew up the decisive report that served as the basis for what at the time was called the "European Economic Community" of six. His European convictions were unshakeable. In 1956, he wrote, "Together with a number of others, I have for years been convinced of the necessity of combining Europe's strengths, both to find a solution for certain political problems, such as that of Germany, and to give fresh vigour to our divided economies. I do not doubt that the future belongs to the great human communities," adding, "Where there is the political will, there are no insurmountable problems."

The Christian Democrat Pierre Harmel, Foreign Minister, and the Liberal Jean Rey, Chairman of the European Commission from 1967 to 1970, followed in his footsteps. In their turn, they worked hard at constructing the new Europe. Moreover, both pleaded for the admission of the United Kingdom to the European Economic Community. "If someone in a frock-coat and a bowler hat knocks at one's door, one doesn't run up to the first floor to throw a bucket of water over him," exclaimed Jean Rey, albeit mockingly. It was not until 1 January 1973 that his wish was granted. However, Rey will go down in history chiefly as the first president of a real European Community, set up after the merger in 1967 of its three great pillars, the European

Jean Rey, a liberal, was the first president of a truly European Commission.
AMSAB

Economic Community, the European Coal and Steel Community and Euratom.

The present generation appears to have been treading the same path as these three figures. Four names spring to mind. Jean-Luc Dehaene, Christian Democrat Prime Minister, had built up such a reputation as a "plumber", that a majority of European countries wanted to see him become the new president of the European Commission in succession to Jacques Delors, but the veto of the British was eloquent, their fear of his federalist aspirations too great. The Socialist Karel Van Miert, from 1995 to 1999 European Commissioner responsible for competition policy, was one of the few blameless members of Jacques Santer's team and was able to shed his Belgian ways and play an important part in the development of the Economic Union. Lastly, Guy Verhofstadt, the current Prime Minister, and Louis Michel, his Liberal Foreign Minister, showed at the Nice Summit in December 2000 that Belgium's European convictions were still totally intact at the turn of the century. Both have fought to prevent the Union dissolving into a single, great free trade zone upon enlargement. Furthermore, both were among the first to take action against the inclusion of the Far Right in the Austrian government. Little Belgium has always made her voice heard in the international concert. Country of passage, border country. Link country, pure and simple.

Guy Verhofstadt, the current prime minister, attaches great importance to the 'European' concept.
© Van Parys Media

Belgians and Europe

Belgians have Europe's best interests at heart, or at least the Belgian chefs certainly do. What else could the question – half joking, half in total earnest – (often overheard at one of those countless receptions) in the élite world of the EU institutions be referring to: "How many kilos have you been in Brussels?"

Anyone using the names of streets, squares and stations in Brussels as a yardstick for Belgian Euro-enthusiasm, rather than the culinary delights, might well reach a different conclusion. It would be unjustifiably harsh to assume that the gloomy station named after Robert Schuman, one of Europe's founders, really reflects the capital's esteem for the Union. The area in front of the Central Station, sporting the promising name Carrefour de l'Europe, functioned for many a long decade as nothing more than a large car park. Not until the 1980s were any of the debatably aesthetic hotels erected. Apart from tourists, professional Europeans come here to have fun while strolling through the European capital. And we shouldn't forget the unwelcoming street bearing the noble name Boulevard de l'Europe – which has dragged on as a building site for years, right in front of the Brussels South Station.

The names of squares or avenues were nonetheless selected with care. Europe itself has also lingered on as a building site, while over the years its face has changed dramatically: from the former European Community for Coal and Steel (ECCS), through the European Economic Community (EEC) and the European Union (EU) with the unified monetary system, to the embryonic extended Greater Community embracing some 27 members.

Brussels, too, has evolved over time, and certainly not only because of Europe. The city has also adapted its appearance: it has done this often and not necessarily to its advantage. With its architectonic and cultural diversity – the proportion of foreigners is about 30 per cent – Brussels appears to be becoming increasingly similar to a miniature version of the ever more colourful EU. Although many Belgian and foreign inhabitants place the responsibility for escalating property prices and the changes in the city's appearance squarely on 'Europe's' shoulders, it does not alter the fact that the typical civilian feels uninvolved in united thinking. Politicians in all parts of the country are convinced that federal Belgium's future is best served by a federally structured Europe. The Eurosceptic, so widespread elsewhere, is seen here as an exotic species. Belgian politicians support Europe.

Michael Stabenow
Correspondent for the European Union.

Louis Michel, minister for Foreign Affairs, together with his prime minister, makes energetic efforts to command respect for the smaller member states within Europe.
© Nathalie Bidoul

Introducing Belgium. The Country as a Mirror of its People

Belgium? An Island Of Flashing Lights

Seen from the sky — from the moon, even — Belgium is an island of light. The rational explanation for this is the street-lamps that line the Belgian road network, one of the densest and most lit in the world. But what if we allowed our imagination to speak, as the artists of this hub of dreams do? What if that light was much more the expression of the country's energy and creativity?

Without always being conscious of them, Belgium has a substantial number of trump cards to enable her to enter the 21st century with optimism. Her multiplicity of languages and cultures open wide the doors of globalisation. Her resourcefulness and ingenuity place her in a good position to participate actively in the knowledge society. Her pragmatism and good humour allow her to surmount crises with a smile.

The Belgians have no reason for self-doubt. Their only fear is that the fragile institutional structure will one day just collapse. A few years ago, on the Brussels-Lille motorway, one could still read the message, "The last one to leave Belgium, please turn off the light." – a wonderful example of self-mockery for a country that so far has held solidly to its course.

37

Belgian motorways are without doubt the best illuminated in the whole world. Marc Eyskens, the minister of State, years ago quipped that two things on earth would be very clearly visible from space: the Great Wall of China and the Belgian motorways by night. Many people took this as truth, and a new myth was born ...
© Paul De Malsche

A Belgian Existence

Life As It Is

Marie-Anne Wilssens

To be born in Belgium. Just imagine it! You arrive in a pocket-sized little country, which, would you believe, achieved its independence through a revolt set in motion by an aria in grand opera. So not a mere operetta republic, but an operatic kingdom. A land of chips, of chocolates, of live and let live; a flat land, a hilly land, a wet land, a small land and a grand land, a land of heroes, a grotesque land, a let's-drink-to-it land, a the-branches-of-your-tree-are-hanging-over-the-garden-wall land, a land of compromises, a the-situation-is-hopeless-but-not-serious land, a mystic land, a Catholic land, an anti-religious land, an open land, a clear-off land, a comic strip land, a fearfully complicated land.

But pleased to see you, little Belgian.

40

The Royal Mint Theatre in Brussels, by the architect Louis-Emmanuel-Aimé Damesme, dates from the late eighteenth century. It was there, during a performance of Auber's La Muette de Portici, that the revolt broke out which led to the creation of Belgium. In recent years the present 'Munt Schouwburg' or 'Théâtre Royal de la Monnaie' has gained an international reputation as an opera house.

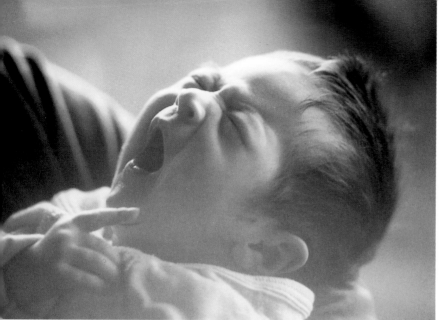

Born In Fascinating Belgium
Welkom! Bienvenue! Wilkommen! Welcome!

Every new Belgian is welcome, and this in spite of the fact that Belgium is one of the most densely populated countries in the world. With 333 inhabitants per square kilometre, Belgium is as crowded as Japan. Only the Dutch, with their 376 inhabitants per square kilometre, are more crowded

That every new-born infant is received with open arms can not only be ascribed to the fact that Belgians love children, but also to the fear that soon there will not be enough workers to cover the cost of pensions. Belgium has a system by which pensions are not paid out of a funded reserve, but from the contributions of those in work and their employers. Since all the Baby Boomers will be retiring in the foreseeable future, there must be enough younger Belgians to make sure that the extra costs of pensions and the care of the sick and the aged can be paid.

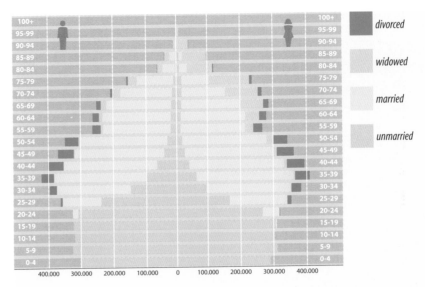

NIS: graph of the population pyramid

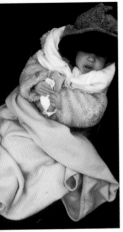

Rich Belgian, Or Not So Rich Belgian?

Anyone born in Belgium need not worry too much about their material prospects. The likelihood of their being poor is small. Belgium has a poverty rate of 5.8 per cent, the lowest figure in the world after Finland. This favourable situation can be ascribed to a well-thought-out and efficient social security system.

Anyone born in Belgium had at this moment in time best do so in the Brussels Metropolitan Region or the province of Antwerp, respectively fourth and tenth in the pecking order of the most wealthy regions of Europe. West Flanders is interesting, too. The Walloon Region, still struggling with the social consequences of the decline of its old industrial activities, scores 88 per cent of the European average.

42

Regional Gross Domestic Product per head in parities of purchasing power (average 1995-1997- EU 15 = 100)	
Belgium	112
Brussels Metropolitan Region	170
Flemish Region	115
Antwerp	138
Limburg	109
East Flanders	104
Flemish Brabant	97
West Flanders	116
Walloon Region	88
Hainault	80
Liège	99
Luxemburg	96
Namur	86
Walloon Brabant	88

Source: Eurostat

43

A Welcoming Gift

A birth is a joyful event and the government is perfectly willing to recognize it as such. For a birth the parents receive a maternity allowance of more than BEF 38,000 (EUR 942). After that the child has the right to a supplementary family allowance, popularly known as a "child allowance", up to the age of 25 or until he or she starts earning. This applies to every child, whether born to the checkout girl at the supermarket or the general manager of a multinational corporation. The amount varies depending on whether the child is the first, second, third or a later child. The self-employed have their own system within social security. They, too, get a family allowance, though it is lower than that of wage earners.

The Child Must Have A Name

Every child born in Belgium is automatically given their father's surname, though there are growing voices for the choice to be left to the parents. In any case a child can expect to have a 'Belgian' surname. That means either a French one or a Flemish one. The most common surnames are Peters, Janssens and Maes in Flanders, and Dubois, Lambert, Dupont and Dumont in the French-speaking areas.

A substantial proportion of French-speakers have a Flemish surname. This is mainly the result of the migration of Flemings who moved to the Walloon Region to work in the mines or the steel mills. It is estimated that during the 19th century and the first half of the 20th, between 500,000 and 1 million Flemings moved to the Walloon Region. Anyone looking at the telephone directory of a town such as Charleroi is amazed at the large number of people called Janssens or Peters, or who have a name beginning with Van.

Ludwig Van Beethoven was of Belgian ancestry.
© Paul De Malsche

Ludwig Van Beethoven, If You Please

The most famous Van is probably Ludwig Van Beethoven. Ludwig was the grandson of Lodewijk, a chorister and organist from Malines who emigrated to Bonn to work in the Elector's choir. His marriage to a Bonn girl resulted in the birth of a son, Johann. He in turn became a musician, and the father of Ludwig, who as the eldest son was according to tradition blessed with his grandfather's Christian name, translated into German.

In Germany the 'Van' of Van Beethoven was transformed into 'von', a prefix implying an aristocratic origin. The Flemish 'van' usually only indicates the place from which someone comes or where he lives. Someone who came from Brussels would be called Van Brussel, and similarly there are people called Van Antwerpen or Van Gent. The ancestors of Jean-Claude Van Damme came from a small place called Damme. Other 'Vans' refer to the location of their house. Someone who lived on a hill was called Van de Berg, Van den Berghe or Van den Heuvel. The first Van Beethoven was probably a man who came from a hamlet called Beethove (Bettehove).

Ludwig Van Beethoven was quite happy to be addressed as 'von'. He is not the only person who played around with his "van". Many Flemings, inspired by the French 'de', began to write their "van" with a small v to give the impression that they were of noble birth. The Dutch with 'van' in their names have always written it with a small v.

There are also Flemings who have a French name, but their number is much smaller than the Walloons who acquired their name from a Flemish forebear. You can't tell from a surname whether someone is Flemish or French-speaking. A Christian name is a better guide, though there, too, the boundary between the languages is not always clear.

A Belgian Named Dylan

The time when a child was named after a godfather or godmother, and every family was full of people called Jan or Louis, often with the same surname, is long past. As is the time when fathers arrived at the registry office so merry that with the best will in the world they could not remember what name had been agreed for the child. This does not prevent plenty of Belgians walking around now with a Christian name they hate because their father's memory had failed him when he got to the registrar. Fortunately those who are unhappy with their name and have a good reason, can now change their Christian name quite cheaply. A name which is manifestly ridiculous or objectionable can be changed for BEF 2,000. Less 'essential' name changes cost ten times as much.

Among the children born in 1999, more than a thousand girls acquired the name Laura, while 941 little Belgian boys were blessed with the name Thomas. The classic names also do well in the top ten. For girls Marie, Sarah, Manon, Julie, Lisa, Charlotte, Emma and Camille are the leaders. Among boys, names such as Nicolas, Maxime, Lucas, Louis, Simon and Antoine are strongly represented. Robin is an intruder and this is even more the case with Dylan, a name which parents gave their little son in 469 cases.

Football, too, has inspired the choice of Christian names. Kevin Keegan may have retired from active playing for some time, but that did not prevent 293 sets of parents naming their son after him. Johan Cruyff's son, Jordi, inspired 257 parents. While the tendency to name children after TV stars or football heroes applies to both sides of the language border, among Flemings there is also a fashion for digging up old Flemish names, such as Dries, Michiel, Stijn, Maarten, Nele, Fien, Kaat and Tine, or to bestow Scandinavian or Frisian names on their children, such as Jens, Arne, Jarne, Niels, Silke, Femke, Britt and Bo. Among French-speakers Celtic or Celtic-sounding names have been the fashion for some years. There are a number of Dorians and Florians running around.

That the name Mohammed is number 38 in the top hundred is of course a sign of the times. And that ecology and New-Age values have also influenced the names Belgians give their children is evident from the 333 Océanes, the 249 Marines and the 185 Lunas.

Already A Small Citizen

You are a Belgian as soon as your father, your mother, or both of them register your birth at the registry office in the Town Hall. They have 15 days to do this. Leave it too long and you can expect a legal prosecution and a fine. The parents must take a whole wad of documents with them: their identity cards, their marriage certificate if they are married, or if necessary a form acknowledging the child as their own if they are not married. Around 15 per cent of births in Belgium are of children born outside wedlock. Another essential document is a certificate from the doctor or midwife who attended the birth.

When all the papers are in order, the official in the registrar's office gives the applicant a sheaf of documents to take home with which the parents can have the child registered for health insurance and with which they can apply for their "child allowance" and "maternity benefits". These documents also include information about inoculations. In Belgium parents are required to have their children inoculated against polio. They must, within a prescribed term, produce evidence for the local authorities that the child has indeed been vaccinated.

Knowing That You Think Is Not Enough

It may have been enough for Descartes to state "I think, therefore I am" but for a Belgian it is rather more complicated. This may be because early in the 20th century a Walloon politician wrote to the King saying, "Sire, there are no Belgians," or because he so often has the feeling of living in a surrealist country, but a Belgian feels the need to prove his existence and identity continually and irrefutably. In concrete terms he is only really happy when it is all down on paper.

Fortunately the bureaucracy makes sure that from his birth onwards he has nothing to fear in that respect. The brand-new parents get an "identity document" for their child. It is a card bearing the child's name and date of birth, contained in a plastic folder provided with a ribbon, so that it can be hung round the neck. In practice it disappears somewhere in a drawer, or in an album, since for the proud parents it is actually the first concrete evidence of the existence of their offspring. Small children can also obtain a "proof of identity". However, this must be applied for specially. The document is essential for children who travel abroad with their parents.

When a child is 12 years old, he or she gets a real identity card.

In adult life, particularly in applications or contacts with the authorities, Belgians often also have to provide an extract from their birth certificate. And if any doubt arises on whether or not someone is still alive or not, the person involved can even obtain a certificate from the Town Hall to prove that he is alive.

The arrival of each new baby is celebrated with *suikerbonen* (sugared sweets), distributed lavishly among family, friends and acquaintances.

A Sweet Ritual

Belgians may have abandoned the old rituals for name-giving, but there is a substantial part of the old traditions which is still honoured. For instance, in the choice of godfathers and godmothers the old pattern is often followed. That means that the father's father and the mother's mother are the first to be asked to be godfather and godmother.

Officially, from time immemorial, the main duty of godfathers and godmothers was to renounce the devil and all his works on behalf of the child, but in practice it is rather different. The most important task of godfathers and godmothers is ... to buy and pass around *suikerbonen* (traditionally sugared almonds) and to give an annual New Year's present until the child is 12 years old.

Suikerbonen, literally 'sugar beans', are now almond-shaped sweets with a chocolate or almond-paste filling. They are packed in a great variety of special boxes or bags.

The sweets are offered to anyone coming to visit the new-born infant. The parents send cards announcing the happy event to family and friends, and at the same time invite them to come and see the baby. Most visitors bring a present of clothes. In Belgium the traditional colours are pink for a girl and blue for a boy. The increased variety of what is on offer has, of course, made this tradition less relevant in recent years. Moreover, more and more parents opt for a "christening list" which is held in a baby wear shop, and consulted by generous donors who can choose in the certainty that the parents will really appreciate their gift.

A Little Water Can Do No Harm

Although fewer and fewer Belgians are themselves churchgoers, a majority of them still have their children christened. About 90 per cent of Belgians are baptised, but only 11 per cent go to Mass every week. Religion only takes fifth place in the Belgian hierarchy of values, after family, friends, leisure time and work. Some 55 per cent of Belgians born since 1970 say they never go to church. This is reflected in a diminishing trend in the number of christenings.

Weekly church	1967	1973	1980	1990	1998
Belgium	42.9	32.3	26.7	17.9	11.2
Flanders	52.0	38.5	32.2	21.3	12.7
Walloon Region	33.9	26.9	21.5	14.6	9.3
Brussels	24.3	16.3	12.0	8.8	6.3

Baptism	1967	1973	1980	1990	1998
Belgium	93.6	89.3	82.4	75.0	64.7
Flanders	96.1	93.6	89.0	83.1	73.1
Walloon Region	92.8	90.3	82.3	74.2	64.8
Brussels	81.6	62.1	44.9	34.4	23.4

Evolution in Participation in Church Services (percentages)   Source: European survey of values

A small proportion of the children who are baptised will later take the trouble to have themselves "unbaptised". Each year there are indeed several hundred Belgians who, once they are adults, decide to have themselves officially registered as not belonging to the Church. Most of those who decide that they do not want to have anything to do with the Church, do nothing about it. They simply decide that their baptism has no meaning for them. In this way they go on contributing to the finances of the Catholic Church because the subsidies for religious services are based on the number of baptisms.

For decades the religious orders have been struggling against the lack of interest of the younger generation, to the extent that some of them have almost ceased to exist.

Personal Perception of Religious Belief in 1996
Percentages relate to the total population

	Belgians	Flemings	French-speakers
Practising believers	21	25	15
Non-practising believers	33	28	39
Practising non-believers	1	1	1
Non-believers, but adhere to religious traditions (baptism, marriage, etc.)	12	16	7
Non-believers, who do not keep to religious traditions	27	25	29
Opposed to all religion	6	5	8

Source: Charles Delhez and Rudolf Rezsohazy, Il est une foi. Valeurs et croyances des Belges.

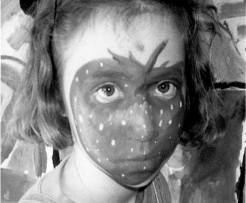

Belgians can be of many colours and countenances. This country is a haven for diverse communities and cultures.

Don't Just Say "Belgian" To A Belgian

One Belgian is not the same as another. That is something foreigners do not always understand. To be a "proper" Belgian, each new-born citizen must also be included in a subcategory, because there must be good order, particularly in a country where people have fought so long for respect for their identity. Every Belgian is therefore also, and in many cases first, a Fleming, Walloon, citizen of Brussels, a German-speaking Belgian or, as a result of recent naturalisation, a 'new Belgian'. A few examples may explain a lot.

Nele was born in Sint-Niklaas. She is Flemish. Loïc and Dries were born in Brussels. They can both claim Brussels citizenship but in the case of Loïc he is very likely to grow up French-speaking, whereas Dries is the son of Flemings and will grow up speaking Dutch.

Quentin was born in Liège and so is plainly Walloon. He will grow up as a French-speaking Belgian. Judith, born in Eupen, has parents who speak German. So she will be a German-speaking Belgian. For Nele it is quite simple. She speaks Dutch and lives in Flanders. That makes her Flemish. Quentin was born in a Walloon area and speaks French. He is a Walloon. Judith is a Walloon because she was born in the Walloon Region, but as a German speaker she comes under the "German Community". Loïc and Dries are both from Brussels, residents of the Metropolitan Region, but one of them is a French-speaking Belgian and the other a Fleming. Their lives will be governed in part by the rules of the Brussels Region where they live, but they belong to different Communities. If Dries goes to a Dutch-speaking school, this will come under the authority of the Flemish Community; if Loïc goes to a French-speaking school, the rules of the French-speaking Community will apply.

Mohammed was born in Ghent. His parents came from Morocco, but a few years ago opted for the "fast-track" Belgian naturalisation process by which they acquired Belgian nationality. Before the law they are ordinary Belgians, but they are labelled as "New Belgians" by the indigenous population. Their small son will actually be regarded in the same way. Mohammed will go to a Flemish school.

Offering childcare is regarded in Belgium as an obvious necessity, not provided in many other countries.

We are talking about the mid-1960s – when I was still a tiny tot. We sat on midget chairs at pink-topped worktables, built plastic towers on a thick rug on the floor, made mountains in our sandbox. On the right, against the classroom wall, were cots where the littlest ones, with their dummies and in their nappies, slept far into the afternoon. After the noon break the second and third-year toddlers folded their arms, let their heads droop and floated bent forwards between dreaming and waking. My generation of 40-plussers must surely remember that. We were barely three and already had a school satchel. In most of the countries round us children did not go to school till they were twice as old.

In Belgium 98 per cent of children are sent to school at about the age of two and a half. Educationists now wonder how it happened that we, just over a generation ago, had already started so early. Was it a side effect of our well-structured primary education system, which had provided a scheme even for the youngest children, or was it that the Catholic schools had nuns with whom parents could safely leave their children? Not for nothing was the pre-school section known as the nursery class.

At that time there was also child care for tinies (from birth to three), though it was not really approved of. While other Western countries had a policy for a pedagogic model for their child care, Belgium, under pressure of the contemporary "National Campaign for Children's Welfare", held on to a medical and hygienic model dating from the inter-war years. Until the 1970s children were still kept in sterile areas with hardly any toys. Tidiness and washing hands were more important than play or talking to the children. There was absolutely no attempt to teach them to do things for themselves.

Child care in Belgium was a disaster, stated the researchers who published Working For Better Child Care in the late 1970s. They kept on about the need for a pedagogic plan. They quoted just one good example: the crèches started by the universities of Ghent, Louvain and Brussels. These did indeed revolve round educational aims. There they did play. But however much they were praised, their impact was still limited.

There was a "boom" around the end of the 1970s when the first child care services within a family environment were organised. They formed host families (childminders) who would look after about five children at home in a home atmosphere. The old-fashioned sterile crèche atmosphere had gone. The 1980s were marked by an extension of these services and an explosive increase in the supply to meet a growing demand. So far Belgium has never suffered from any lack of demand for this kind of child care. On the contrary. Women have to reserve a place for their baby as soon as they become pregnant.

This great demand has everything to do with the Belgian worker (male/female) and particularly with the "/female". In Belgium the term "child care"' is never used outside the context of employment. Within the European Union, too, child care is always thought of as an extension of the concept of equal opportunities for men and women in the labour market. In the Commission's general policy plan of October 2000 we read: "The Commission wants target figures for more child care and an increase in the proportion of women in employment from 51 per cent to 60 per cent, as proposed by the Council of Europe in Lisbon."

Belgium owes its child care – which has meanwhile been professionally structured – to the fact that in Belgium so many women entered the labour market. Under this pressure child care had to organise itself faster and better. In the 1980s women's share of the labour market had already achieved a figure of 40 per cent, while in Germany and the Netherlands these percentages still hovered between 6 and 8 per cent. In Europe Belgium is in second place for the best structured child care, after the front-runner Scandinavia. Partly as a result of our tradition of nursery schools, we have some edge at the pedagogic level, compared with countries such as Germany, the Netherlands and Great Britain, who are bringing up the rear.

Twenty years ago, when the policy of Kind en Gezin (Child and Family) was started, the crèches slowly but surely began to be purged of their purely medical and sterile approach. In addition to nurses and doctors, psychologists and educationists became involved and they stimulated a playful and meaningful environment for the young child.

Day nurseries held on to a smaller market share. Belgian children between the ages of nought and three are mainly taken to childminders and some historians think that the dominance of Catholicism is partly responsible for this. The CVP (Catholic People's Party), unlike its Christian Democratic brothers and sisters in Germany (CDU) or the Netherlands (CDA), has created a positive climate around child care. The religious organisation Caritas, now the Flemish Welfare Union, has much to do with it. More than 12,000 childminders are members of welfare organisations with a denominational allegiance; apart from these there are only 1,700 independent childminders.

In recent years, after the reformation of the day nurseries, another challenge arose: that of the care of children after or out of school. Particularly in the 1980s, when competition between the different types of school was on the increase, this kind of child care was offered to parents as an extra. Disillusion followed quickly when no one could see how to cope with the great demand. For more than 15 years people have been racking their brains how to cope with the adequate expansion of this kind of child care and it worries both educationists and school governors. Teachers themselves are still too involved in after-school child care. It is a bizarre situation. During the day the teachers have the children in class in the context of the transfer of knowledge, and in the evenings they have to play with them. In the past schools sometimes washed their hands of the problem all too easily by just sitting the children down in the classroom, including the infants who had to stay in their seats until mum or dad came to collect them after 5 o'clock. There, too, regional education centres had their work cut out to alter the situation. And, they sigh, we are still not out of the woods, because the out-of-school child-care centres we set up are still small and not properly structured.

So child care in Belgium, despite good initiatives and adequate development, is still a controversial issue. When the policy is criticised, people are still too prone to point to our neighbours in the far north. We are inclined to take them as an example, but perhaps some qualifications should be made. In Sweden, for example, both mothers and fathers are encouraged to keep the child in a parental environment for the first year of life. This has led to a social policy in which the margin between wages and the payments to a parent staying at home is kept very small. It is, however, striking that even Swedish men are a little unwilling to take on the task of housefather. When it proves that it is mainly mothers who care for the child at home, this in fact works against the original aim (to share child care between husband and wife) and weakens the position of women in the labour market.

Perhaps we should end by quoting the African saying that most importantly it takes "a village to raise a child". Bringing up children should at its best occur in the broadest possible interpretation: both in the nuclear family, the extended family, at school, and in organisations outside. Child care should be a comprehensive policy, in which all potential solutions should exist and be supported, a policy which is not constricted by the creation of a few legal provisions.

Marijke Libert
Freelance journalist with the daily De Morgen.

55

Growing Up In Belgium

What Shall We Do With The Little One?

For the first three years of their lives little Belgians are looked after by their own parents or, if both of them are working, by a grandmother, a childminder, or a crèche. There are unofficial childminders, whose names are passed from one mother to another, and there are official childminders, who have to meet quality standards laid down by the authorities. In addition there are crèches, established by the local councils. The fees parents pay for them depend on their incomes. This is also the case when the child is taken to a registered childminder who receives a fee per child from the authorities, part of which is paid by the parents. The parents' expenses for child care are fully tax-deductible.

Know What You Want At The Age Of Three

From the age of three almost all children go to infant school. In this area Belgium leads Europe. As many as 99 per cent of three-year olds already attend a nursery class, and by the time they are four, 100 per cent enter the school doors every day.

When they go to their first school the young Belgians immediately make the acquaintance of a Belgian peculiarity: the different education networks. These are the result of the right written into the Belgian constitution: the right to a free choice of school. It amounts to every Belgian having the opportunity to send his children to a school that matches his convictions.

Although Belgian society is strongly secularised, a majority of parents still opt for the free network that traditionally is biased towards the confessional segment. In French-speaking Belgium 49 per cent of the pupils in primary and secondary education go to a school run by the authorities (the Community). The other 51 per cent go to a school with "free" – in practice Catholic – education, or to a school in the provincial or municipal network. In Flanders 30 per cent go to schools in the official education system and 70 per cent to free ones.

The choice of a particular education network is in most cases made when the child goes to infant school. In Belgium, Community schools and "free" schools are to be found in the same

From the age of three most children
go to school.

districts and even in the same street, and every morning you can see one stream of small children going to one school and another going off in the other direction. Often the infant school is part of a school which also covers primary education, but sometimes it is isolated in a residential area, a kind of outpost of one particular philosophy of life. Some parents choose the easiest solution and take their children to the nearest school, others bypass that building on their way to the institution which matches their conviction.

In Catholic schools children get to hear something about God, and the religious background for holidays such as Easter and Christmas are discussed, but not in the other schools. That most parents, in spite of the fact that often they are not themselves believers, still send their children to a school in the free network, is mainly explained by the fact that they want their children to have something they are familiar with themselves. Quite a few parents think that they have to give their children a package of "Christian education" because Christianity is after all the basis of West-European culture. Others think that their children should get to know about religion "so that later they can choose for themselves". In many cases there is still a conviction that the Catholic schools are "better". There are even parents who send their children to them because in the Catholic education system uniforms are still worn. Of course, parents who want to be consistent and send their offspring to the official education system, think that the others are inconsistent and reinforce a system from which they have for a long time been alienated. Politicians occasionally point out the high cost of the Belgian system, but they then immediately run up against a wall of protest or are told to put a lid on it so as not to reopen any old wounds. The free choice of schools is a sacred cow and anyone who tampers with it disturbs a balance that was achieved after more than a century's argument and strife.

Children attend primary school from the age of six to twelve. From their fifth year of school, in other words, at about the age of ten or eleven, they learn a second language: in Flanders French, in Brussels Dutch or French, in the Walloon Region Dutch or English.

Education in Belgium

Education in Belgium is organised by the Flemish, French and German-speaking Communities and is synonymous with freedom. There is freedom of choice for parents and their children. They can choose a school in function of its proximity or, if so desired, on the basis of philosophical convictions. Only objective reasons, such as lack of space, could be cited for rejecting an application for enrolment.

There are several systems in existence, all of which are financed by the communities. In terms of official education, there are, on the one hand, schools run directly by the communities, whose role in this case is not exclusively that of subsidising authority. On the other hand, there is subsidised official education, organised by the municipalities and provinces. In contrast with this government education,

there is free education. The organising authority here is confessional (mostly Catholic as this faith enjoys a substantial majority) or non-confessional. It is in this last category that schools applying an alternative method of teaching, as developed by Freinet, Hamaide or Decroly, for instance, would be found.

There are a few exceptions relating to freedom of choice: in the municipalities with a special language statute or in the Brussels schools, parents wishing to enrol their children need to fulfil certain linguistic or residential conditions. Pedagogical freedom is a basic principle laid down in the constitution. Those schools in the free system are especially committed to this. It was one of the major points of conflict in the successive phases of the "School Funding Controversy" in which the adherents of free and official education were on opposing sides, until in 1959 the "School Pact" was signed. This pact acknowledges the existence of the two systems, regulates the subsidies and lessons related to the so-called philosophical considerations. In the official education system the pupil can indeed choose between one of the recognised religions or non-confessional ethics. Nevertheless, the pedagogical freedom of the schools is restricted. Each community defines the capabilities required of the pupil and lays down the programme for each school year.

After the compulsory period of education, from 6 to 18 years of age, youngsters can enrol at a university or institute of further education for a course of study of long or short duration. Here again, open enrolment is the most significant characteristic. The student is required only to submit his diploma of higher secondary education. This freedom of enrolment is not totally absolute. For some study areas, entrance examinations are organised or a numerus clausus applied. This is the case for engineering, medicine, dentistry and for certain institutes of further education, especially those offering a course in the arts. These restrictions are minimal, especially in view of the total number of educational options on offer. Free access to further education attracts many students to Belgium from other European countries, where more stringent selection is enforced. For example, at the French-speaking faculties of veterinary science, there are many French students enrolled.

Isabelle Lemal
Journalist with Le Soir.

To The Primary School

After infant school, children go to primary school. There is always enough choice. The choice of school has usually already been made when the children started infant school. Seven out of ten children go to a primary school in the same system. Those who still have to make a choice do so on the basis of their religious convictions, the quality of the school, and how far away it is. The image of the school also has a part to play and among some parents the free schools still have the image of providing better education than the official schools, and having better discipline. Most parents are influenced by what they hear from other parents. The folders and

advertisements published by the schools have little or no influence. For the rest, parents also take into account whether or not hot lunches are served there, if there is an organised school bus service and what arrangements there are for child care before and after school.

In the choice between two schools of about equal advantages, distance is usually the deciding factor. The result is that three children out of four go to a primary school within a radius of three kilometres (two miles) from their home.

No Longer So Catholic

Children who go to a Catholic school will receive religious instruction from their schoolmaster or mistress and will be prepared for their First Communion.

Here, too, customs have changed drastically. After all, the children of atheists or Muslims also attend Catholic schools and the management does not require them to make Communion.

Obviously the official schools think this hypocritical and, moreover, unfair competition. In the official schools the rule is that everyone can receive religious instruction in so far as it concerns a "recognised" religion and that non-believers will have lessons in "non-denominational ethics" instead. "Recognised religions" are those whose ministers are paid by the state. In Belgium there are six recognised religions: Roman Catholic, Anglican, Protestant, Orthodox, Judaism and Islam. Islam is the second most important religion in the country.

So it is possible for parents to express their beliefs in their choice of education for their children. Even those who are believers themselves, but actually think that education should be completely secular, can find a solution to suit them. They can send their child to an official school and let them learn about religion there. Only those belonging to some kind of small sect have a problem. They will have to give their children religious instruction themselves.

After Catholicism the largest religious groups are Islam, Protestantism and Judaism.

DIY Education

In Belgium there is no compulsory education, no compulsory school attendance. This means that parents who do not find a school to their taste can teach their children themselves. The children can obtain an official diploma if they pass an examination set by the Middenjury (Central Examination Board). Adults past school age who decide to study, but do not have the opportunity to attend classes, can also go straight to the Examination Board.

The First Communion

Most Belgian children make their First Communion. If not because they are believers, it will be because they love to organise a party and receive presents. In the past parents used to take their children to visit the family, and the children would be given a present or some pocket money. Now a party is organised to which the family is invited. Communicants leave a wish list in a shop from which their family and friends can choose a gift. Many children get a bicycle on the occasion of their First Communion. For the children of "free-thinkers" a "flower festival" is organised to celebrate the transition from infant school to their first year of "real" school. Religious education itself has also evolved appreciably. Where previously doctrine and devotional history were still the most important part of it, nowadays it all revolves mainly round social questions. There is less lecturing, more discussion. Children learn about and discuss the poverty and the injustices in the world, about discrimination, homosexuality, drugs, the great world religions, AIDS, etc. In this sense religious instruction is intrinsically often very similar to ethics, and not all Catholic parents are happy about this.

English spoken

A foreigner addressing someone in Flanders or in the French-speaking region of the country has more chance of getting an answer if he speaks to them in English than in the other national language. Both among Flemings and French-speakers there are more people who speak English than the second language of the country. Seventy per cent of Flemings think that they are capable of speaking French, while 38 per cent of French-speakers say they know Dutch. Three out of four Brussels citizens say they can speak the other national language.

On both sides of the language border the situation is better as far as knowledge of English is concerned. In Flanders 87 per cent claim to speak English. Some 57 per cent of Flemings say that their English is "more or less faultless". About 44 per cent think this is also true of the quality of their French. Among the Walloon population 65 per cent claim to speak English, among the inhabitants of Brussels 77 per cent.

België Mon Vaterland

In their fifth year of school, when the children are about 11 years old, they are for the first time confronted with a foreign language. In Belgium this is the "second language": in Flanders it is French, in Brussels either Dutch or French. Schoolchildren living in the Metropolitan Region already have to deal with the "other" language from their third year in school. In the Walloon Region children have the choice between Dutch, English or German as their second language. Most choose English.

Flemish children would rather learn English than French, because it is easier for them and "cooler". The quality of French among the Flemings has consequently seriously deteriorated in recent years. Among the French-speakers there is traditionally little enthusiasm for learning Dutch. Parents reason that their children will be better off knowing a major language such as English than a minor language such as Dutch, and so Dutch is chosen only as a third language. Recently, however, there has been a change in this situation and many French-speaking parents have come to realise that it is more useful to learn Dutch first and then English.

Yet Another Communion And More Presents

Pupils make their First Communion and renew their baptismal vows in their sixth year at school, while a "spring festival" is organised for the children of "free-thinkers". In fact this is always a rite of passage to adulthood.

A Little More Of A Citizen Thanks To The Identity Card

From his 12th year a Belgian has to have an identity card with him. Anyone reaching the relevant age gets a notice from their local council that they must fill in a form and bring some passport photos. They submit these to the council office and a little later he or she can go back for their identity card. It is by no means a traumatic event. A Belgian is not weighed down by the fact that he has to carry this card on him. For a 12-year old it is an attribute showing that he is being taken more seriously, and adults think it normal and even an advantage to carry something with which they can prove who they are. Belgians involved in an automobile accident show each other their identity cards. This establishes their identity and makes it much more difficult for those concerned to escape their responsibility. An identity card is also convenient if anyone has trouble spelling your name. You do not have to start spelling it out, just pull the card from your pocket. Admittedly showing an identity card can be embarrassing when it is the police who ask for it. Then it can mean that you have either infringed some rule or other, or else that the police think you look a bit suspect. It is at these moments that the naturally very anarchic Belgian feels a great resentment against the obligation to carry his identity card with him, and against the authority that has burdened him with this.

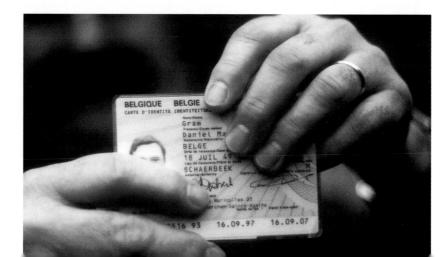

A Present From Germany

Belgians have long forgotten that identity cards are actually a remnant of the First World War, when the country was occupied by Germans, who in 1916 decided that everyone must have an identity card with their photo. The male population had to report each month to the Kommandatur with their cards. Photographers did not bemoan the extra work, but other Belgians did not think much of it. They constantly managed to "lose" their cards. The occupiers found themselves obliged to introduce severe punishment for the loss of the document to encourage the obstinate Belgians to be more careful.

A Child's Year Of Happiness

Sinterklaas

In the course of the year Belgian children have several highlights to look forward to. The date most eagerly awaited is 6 December, the feast of St Nicholas or Sinterklaas. Belgium, like the Netherlands and Switzerland, is a Sinterklaas country, not a Santa Claus country. St Nicholas is often portrayed with three children in a tub. The legend is that the holy bishop of Myra (in Turkey) came to an inn where the landlord had just murdered three children, cut them up and pickled them. The holy man found out about it, blessed the tub, and the children were restored to life, with all the bits back in the right place. This explains why he is the patron saint of children.

Sinterklaas has a black servant, Zwarte Piet (Black Peter), and rides on his horse or donkey over the roofs. He comes down the chimney into the houses and leaves presents. These are not only toys, but also sweets, particularly chocolate and marzipan figures. Spiced biscuits, rather like gingerbread, in the shape of Sinterklaas, and mandarin oranges are also a traditional part of the feast. Children leave letters with a list of wishes by the hearth, with a turnip or a carrot for the Saint's horse or donkey. Children on both sides of the language border know a whole list of

St Nicholas is the children's great
friend, who spoils them all on 6
December with sweets and toys.
© Paul De Malsche

St Nicholas appears in many shapes
and sizes. Traditionally his image is
often made of speculaas, a kind of
gingerbread.

Sinterklaas songs, which they sing all the time. When he is not in Belgium bringing presents, legend has it that the Saint lives in Spain. That is where the mandarins and oranges which he brings grow.

Belgium would not be Belgium if there were no exceptions to the rule. In the middle of St Nicholas's territory there are some enclaves where St Martin performs a similar function. In those regions the children are already celebrating by 11 November.

Santa Claus

While the old tradition of Sinterklaas is honoured undiluted, interest is growing in a foreign import: Santa Claus. The older generation looks askance at this. He tends to symbolise the excessive commercialisation of life. Moreover, Santa Claus is actually an Americanised version of Sinterklaas, who was introduced to North America by the Dutch settlers. So the figure of Santa Claus is the result of the Dutch colony there and his name is a corruption of Sinterklaas. Santa Claus therefore duplicates the event.

But in spite of the reservations of many older people, the advance of Santa Claus is unstoppable. He can no longer be barred from window displays and shopping centres. In recent years he has started to appear several weeks before Christmas, so that his presence has overlapped with that of Sinterklaas. This was really too much of a good thing for everyone. Parents complained that their children's sense of time was turned completely upside down. So agreements have recently been made with shops and department stores. Now there must be no advertising for Sinterklaas and the Easter Bunny more than six weeks before the actual holidays, and Santa Claus may not appear before 1 December at the earliest. In the end, however, it makes very little difference and the fact remains that Belgian children now expect a present for Christmas, too.

A New Year, Another Holiday

After Christmas comes New Year. That is an important date for children too. It begins on New Year's Eve. First an abundance of food and drink is consumed, and at midnight there is champagne and fireworks. Antwerp offers an additional attraction. There all the ships in the harbour sound their hooters at midnight. At that moment anyone within sight or sound of Antwerp opens his window to listen for the wind bringing the New Year wishes of foreign sailors.

As in many other European countries, Belgian living rooms are adorned with richly decorated Christmas trees.

On New Year's Day there is more celebrating, usually at the grandparents' home. Uncles, aunts and cousins are all there. Because grandparents are usually also the godparents, children have

Half a century ago a gingerbread heart was a standard New-Year's present. They are still sometimes given out of nostalgia. The term 'gingerbread heart' is also used locally as a metaphor for a 'tender heart'.

to read their "New Year letter" to them. For shy children this is a real ordeal, and they hurry through it as fast as they can. Children who cannot yet read learn a script by heart at infant school. That is pasted onto the inside of the letter by their teacher and the children pretend to be actually reading it.

Reading the letter full of good wishes and New Year's resolutions is an essential condition for receiving a New Year's present. This may be a bag of sweets with a nice bit of pocket money, or a toy. Many godparents like to honour an old tradition by adding a large "peperkoek" (a kind of gingerbread) to all this. Sometimes this is made in a heart shape or has a little chocolate figure on top. In the past many families were doomed to eat peperkoek until well past Easter before all traces of the New Year had disappeared. The drop in the birth-rate has at least helped to cure that problem.

The Wise Men From The East

Hot on the heels of the New Year comes the holiday of Twelfth Night. Traditionally children dress up and carry a stick with a star on top from house to house, singing carols. In return they receive some fruit, sweets, or a little money from the people in the houses. The number of children who still take the trouble to dress up and blacken their faces to play at being Melchior, Caspar and Balthazar has, however, greatly declined.

'Singing the three kings' is an old tradition that still survives today. On and around 6 January children dressed up as the three wise men go from door to door singing carols. In return for their sometimes rather hesitant singing they are given a few coins or sweets.
© Paul De Malsche

Easter is a happy time for children too. Then the 'bells' come home 'from Rome', dropping delicious chocolate eggs in their flight.

The Bells Come Home From Rome

After Twelfth Night there is a long wait before the next opportunity to celebrate, but at last it is Easter. Time for the Easter bells. Belgians are familiar with the Easter Bunny, but they associate Easter eggs with the "Bells of Rome". The story children are told is that at three o'clock on Good Friday, the time Christ died on the cross, all the bells in church towers go away to Rome. There they collect eggs from the Pope and on Easter Saturday fly home again. By Sunday morning they are back over their own country and start the descent, to take up their places in their own church towers. As they fly low they drop the Easter eggs in people's gardens. It is easy to explain why the eggs are never broken: it is a miracle. The story of the Bells of Rome rests on the tradition that the bells in the church towers fall silent from Good Friday and only sound again at the moment that Christ rose again from the dead. The bells bring the children not only chocolate eggs, but also toys. They are mostly things that can be used to play with outside – it is after all nearly summer – and often include a ball.

Holidays!

Easter, like Christmas, means a two-week holiday. At the end of June the long summer holiday starts and schools close their doors for two months. There have sometimes been arguments about this long holiday. It all goes back to the time when children had to help their parents in the summer with the harvest, and so has little relevance to the needs of schoolchildren in the early 21st century.

An attempt to make holidays start at different times in Flanders and the Walloon Region was abandoned after several years. The idea was to please the hotel and restaurant owners on the coast, who complained that their establishments were full to overflowing for short periods, but afterwards lay largely empty. By spreading the holidays the peak periods would last longer and the load would be better distributed. Practice proved this wrong. The tourist trade complained that their costs remained the same, while their businesses were only half full. Since then Flanders and the Walloon Region go on holiday at the same time.

To break up the long period between the start of the school year in September and the Christmas holiday, there is one week of "autumn holiday" on the occasion of All Saint's Day (1 November). At the end of February the long Easter term is interrupted for a week by the "Crocus holiday".

Secondary School

Once children have their primary school diploma in their pocket, they have to choose a secondary school. In practice it is almost always the parents who make the choice. This depends, even more than the choice of a primary school, on their religious convictions. Six out of ten parents deliberately choose a denominational school. Distance does not weigh so heavily, though half the parents do tend to choose a school which the children can reach by bicycle.

In fact there is seldom a real problem. After all, there is no shortage of supply in secondary education. In Flanders, for example, within a radius of 12 kilometres, you can always find at least one secondary school or comprehensive school. Half the pupils in secondary education have to

go no further than five kilometres, and the rest go to a school between five and 15 kilometres away.

Most children are taken to school by car. The others either have a season ticket on public transport, or go to school by bicycle. In the flat Flanders country one in three children bicycles to school. In Brussels and the Walloon Region bicycles are used less. Brussels children use the tram or the metro more frequently, while in the Walloon Region the car is the most frequent mode of transport between home and school.

A Diploma For Eight Out Of Ten

The choice of school naturally also depends on the curriculum offered by the institution. Most children take the ASO (General Secondary Education). This kind of education is chosen by 35 per cent of the boys and 45 per cent of the girls. Technical education is chosen by 36 per cent of boys and 28 per cent of girls. The remainder mainly take vocational courses.

On the whole secondary education in Belgium is in pretty good shape. About eight out of every ten 22-year olds have a secondary education diploma. This puts Belgium in fourth place in the EU.

A Heavy Programme: Sex And Drugs And Rock 'n Roll

Between the ages of 12 and 18 youngsters do not only acquire academic learning. This is the time when they first fall in love, drink their first pint, learn to drive a car or a motor scooter, and probably enjoy their first cigarette or joint. They will also perhaps vote for the first time.

To Do Or Not To Do "It"

By the age of 15 about 16 per cent of young Belgians have had sex. By 17 between 50 and 60 per cent have done "it" once, two years later that goes for 90 per cent. Boys on average begin six months younger than girls. Young people taking vocational or technical courses are quicker to

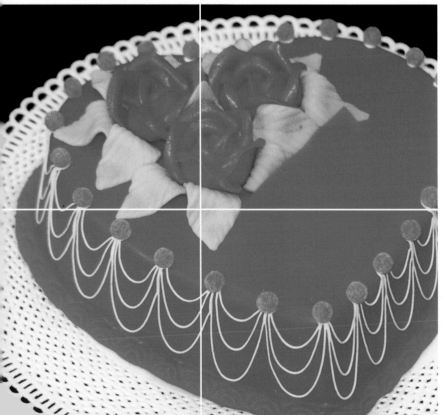

Valentine's day, the lovers' feast on the fourteenth of February, has in recent years become increasingly observed in Belgium.

do so than those enrolled in general secondary education. Most teenagers practise relatively safe sex. About 80 per cent use a condom or the pill. The others try to reduce the risk by less reliable methods, such as coitus interruptus or periodic abstinence, or take no precautions at all. Only 20 per cent protect themselves both against pregnancy and against sexually transmitted diseases by combining the pill and a condom.

The number of pregnancies among girls less than 15 years old is very low. In 1997, 47 girls under the age of 15 had abortions, and among girls between 15 and 19 years old 1,744 pregnancies were terminated.

Few Teenage Mothers

Belgium has relatively few teenage mothers. In comparison with other European countries it is in the middle range in this area. The number of teenage mothers per thousand girls in the relevant age categories is in fact declining. At the moment it is around 7.7. The decline must be set against the growing number of teenage abortions, particularly among 15 and 16-year old girls.

Age	1993	1994	1995	1996	1997	1998	1999
-15	35	48	41	37	46	58	33
15	91	101	123	143	133	145	144
16	153	191	239	253	249	267	301
17	272	275	324	369	369	416	417
18	323	351	380	481	455	457	511
19	411	418	454	544	538	496	616
Total	1,285	1,384	1,561	1,827	1,790	1,839	2,022

Number of Abortions per Age Group   Source: NIS

Mother At A Young Age

Most births among younger women are the result of a desired pregnancy. Particularly in less well-off families and among non-indigenous ones, women have their first child at a young age. Among non-indigenous women the average age at the birth of their first child is 22, apprecia-

Adolescents have plenty to learn, including about sex. Part of their information on this comes from their parents, part from school, but most from the media.

77

bly lower than the national average. Only a small number of children are given away for adoption at birth. In 1998 the total was 40 children.

Sex Education

Sex education is and remains a thorny problem. Belgians do not talk about sex easily. Young people only gather their knowledge from their parents to a small extent. It is usually the mother who is landed with the task. In general young people feel that their parents talk too much about the dangers and too little about other aspects. In the end most of their information comes from magazines and books, and from radio or TV. Friends are particularly good at chatting about sexual experiences. At school the youngsters learn mainly the technical aspects: reproduction, contraception and hygiene.

Although sex education is not a compulsory part of the curriculum, most school boards and teachers think that it is the school's job to enlighten children on that aspect of life. Lessons are given by teachers of religion or non-denominational ethics or by the biology staff. Sometimes external specialists from organisations such as the Centre for Family Planning and Sex Education are called upon.

Research suggests that most teaching staff do not exactly volunteer to give sex education. They feel insecure and sometimes have difficulty with the reactions of the children. They also find it annoying that their pupils often seem to know more about the subject than they do themselves. Seven out of ten youngsters appear to be dissatisfied with the sex education they receive at school

Drinking, Smoking, Drugs

In the time at secondary school young Belgians may also be introduced to drinking, smoking and the use of drugs. Research in Flanders among children from 12 to 18 indicates that in the past year one in three has smoked, three out of four have drunk alcohol, and one in six has used drugs.

Among 12-year-olds one in ten drinks strong drink or alcopops (a mixture of strong drink and soft drinks). They drink mostly beer; alcopops are the second most popular alcoholic drink. Among those who drink beer, 60 per cent are regular drinkers, suggesting that they imbibe at least once a week.

Among drugs, cannabis is the most used. Two per cent of 13-year-olds already use it; among 18-year-olds this figure has gone up to 35 per cent. Ecstasy, the classic party drug, is already used by 1 to 2 per cent of 14-year-olds and by 8 per cent of 18-year-olds, and cocaine by 1 per cent of 15-year-olds and 4 per cent of 18-year-olds. With those figures Belgium is still a relatively drug-free country. In any case about two-thirds of drug use is occasional and it appears that about one in four young people who have used drugs at some time, have

In Belgium at the age of sixteen you may ride a motor scooter, go to a pub without being accompanied by an adult, or have sex.

stopped.

The government recently decided to amend the law on the possession and use of drugs. If the new law is approved by Parliament, the use of cannabis and the possession of a small quantity of it by adults will no longer be an offence, except if the user disturbs public order or the use leads to addiction problems. Dealing in drugs will still be a criminal offence.

Reaching Sixteen

Sixteen has a special meaning for young people. From that age they are allowed to ride a motor scooter or go to a café (the Belgian equivalent of a pub) or disco unaccompanied. Of course many of them do not wait until they reach this magic age to go and drink a Coke in a café with their friends after school or to pop into a disco at the weekend.

Sixteen is also the age at which young people are legally allowed to have sex. Sex with someone under 16 is still an offence, even, for instance, when it involves a boy of 16 having intercourse with a girl of 14. Sex with anyone under 14 is in law still considered rape. Sex with someone between 14 and 16 is classed as "indecent assault", but in practice this has for a long time not led to prosecution, except when it involves sex between an adult and a minor. There has for some time been talk of amending the law to match the reality, and of bringing the age of consent down to 14.

Eighteen At Last!

At 18 Belgians reach majority. With their 18th birthday also comes the right to vote, to start a business, to marry, to drive a car, and so on. Eighteen was in the past also the age at which boys were called up for national service, but this was abolished several years ago. Belgium now has a professional army.

Eighteen still remains the minimum age for marriage. In special cases exceptions can be allowed to this rule. However, no marriages are allowed under the age of 16. And you have to get a driving licence before you can drive a car.

Reaching eighteen means a lot. This
is the age at which you can vote,
drive a car, and get married.

In the many wars waged by the Roman general Julius Caesar, the various Belgian tribes gave him the hardest time. He was only able to conquer them because – even then – they were divided amongst themselves. Yet he described the Belgians as "the bravest of all the Gauls".

Many more occupations would follow Caesar's – by Germanic tribes, Vikings, Franks, Burgundians, Spaniards, Austrians, Dutchmen and modern Germans. "And the latest occupier is the government," quips Herman De Croo, who presides over the Belgian Parliament.

It may not be meant seriously, but it is still the best way to sum up how the Belgians think of their government. Not like the Dutch, for whom the government is the protector of their interests, creating order out of the chaos of society. For the average Belgian the government is there to make life difficult, to make him pay too many taxes and fines, to impose all kinds of ridiculous regulations, and above all, to live at his expense. Because, it needs to be said, Belgian civil servants are legion. Almost one Belgian in every ten works for the government and not always efficiently, enthusiastically or obligingly.

Because of all those foreign armies who have marched over them, Belgians have come to see the government as an opponent who is best led down the garden path, whether it is a matter of declaring your income or building a house. The greatest shock wave ever to have hit the country was when, in the 1990s, the government decided to enforce the laws on environmental planning. When the first of thousands of illegally built houses in conservation areas was demolished, there was almost a revolution. The press was full of it and most commentators thought it was "just not on".

The Prime Minister has now conceived the vain plan of ending the politicising of the government forever, and establishing a "model state" in Belgium which will work efficiently and guarantee ideal public service. There is no Belgian who believes that this will ever happen. Even the Premier seems to be aware of how deep-rooted the aversion is to the government, because when he was asked which minister he admired most, he unhesitatingly named the minister in charge of the Civil Service. He is the one who has to sort things out.

Not for nothing did he name his plan for reform after the great scientist Copernicus, who was the first to establish that the earth went round the sun and not the sun round the earth. The minister must now arrange for the government to revolve around the citizen. Not the other way round.

Luc van der Kelen
Columnist for the daily Het Laatste Nieuws.

81

Obliged To Have An Opinion

Belgians not only have the right to vote but the obligation to do so. At every election some 7.3 million adult Belgians are summoned to register their votes. Anyone who does not vote without good reason has to pay a fine which can run up to BEF 5,000. Those who have a good reason for not going to the polls, for instance, if they are sick or abroad, must prove this by producing a certificate from their doctor, travel agent, etc. If they cannot vote themselves, they can authorise their spouse or a close relative to vote in their place. No one can authorise more than one person to vote for them.

What Belgians like least about elections is that they can be summoned to act as an official at a polling station or to count the votes afterwards. Every election provides evidence of how ingenious some Belgians are in avoiding their obligations. Recently the government has been taking stronger action against these obstinate citizens and sometimes substantial fines have been imposed.

Elections are always held on Sunday. The tradition is that whoever presides over the polling station or the counting treats his colleagues to sandwiches or cake. Those who are summoned to act as officials or tellers are paid a small fee. In recent years more and more voting has been done by computer. To give older people the opportunity to become familiar with this method of voting, computers on which they can practise are set up in Town Halls some weeks before the election. Voting by computer resolves some of the problem of finding tellers, but has led to arguments about the reliability of the election results.

Not only compulsory voting, but also the size of some of the ballot papers characterise Belgian elections. This is particularly the case in Brussels where there are both French-speaking and Dutch-speaking parties standing. There are 13 parties in the federal Parliament. There is a maximum limit to the amount of money parties and individual candidates may spend on election publicity.

In the 1999 Parliamentary elections six per cent of voters submitted blank papers. The desirability of compulsory voting has for a long time been under discussion. Some people think that the abolition of compulsory voting would be to the disadvantage of the parties on the far right.

	never or usually not justified	neither justified nor unjustified	usually or always justified
Homosexuality	21.7%	21.8%	56.5%
Prostitution	43.0%	37.6%	19.4%
Suicide	42.1%	36.4%	22.5%
Abortion	30.7%	41.8%	27.5%
Euthanasia at the patient's request	11.1%	21.6%	67.3%
Euthanasia at the request of the family	29.7%	36.6%	33.6%
Killing in self-defence	11.9%	29.7%	58.4%
Divorce	14.1%	39.6%	46.3%

The values with which Belgium's young people start their adult life are evident from a survey by the VUB among students in Flanders in their final year of secondary education.
Opinions of Young People on Sexual Morality and Bio-Ethics(in percentages)

On Their Own Two Feet

After secondary school the young Belgians suddenly find they have acquired a large amount of freedom, either because they start work and become financially independent, or else because they go on to higher education and live in digs.

The young people who can fend for themselves can live alone, or live with a friend. They can also, if the job pays well enough, buy a small car and smart clothes, and visit the disco and the cinema every week. Those who do not find a job immediately, register as job seekers and after nine months can get an unemployment allowance. If they have worked a sufficient number of days, they are entitled to an unemployment benefit. They can take advantage of several government schemes in which they can take additional training courses or in which employers obtain certain incentives to employ young people.

Introducing BOB

To reduce the number of road accidents at weekends, a campaign has been started to prevent young people (or anyone else) getting behind the wheel in a drunken state. For some years the mythical figure of Bob has existed. "Bob" (short for Bewust Onbeschonken Bestuurder – deliberately sober driver) is the one person in a group of merrymakers who has been designated to stay sober and bring everyone home safely. While Bob drinks water or Coke, his or her friends can indulge in a pint or something stronger to their heart's content.

The 'Bob' logo has become the standard symbol of the government campaigns promoting safe, and above all, sober driving.
(Photo: Nationaal Instituut voor Verkeersveiligheid)

Those who go on to higher education have to lead a fairly quiet life as they still have to be maintained by their parents. A university student in digs costs an average BEF 140,000 (EUR 3,471) per year, and at a *hogeschool* (technical university) BEF 147,000 (EUR 3,644). Students who commute from home still cost their parents BEF 70,000 (EUR 1,735) if they go to a university, and BEF 82,000 (EUR 2,033) for a *hogeschool*. These are amounts which can weigh heavily on a family budget, even for people with a good income. At the time that their children go to university, parents are often at a difficult stage in the economic life cycle. They may be earning a lot, but the house will not be completely paid off yet. Or perhaps one of them has already been written off by the labour market as being too old, and is consequently unemployed or has taken early retirement. Moreover, parents usually have more than one child going on to higher education. When middle-aged Belgians complain about their finances and in doing so let drop the words "children in digs", they can immediately rely on all possible sympathy from their audience. *Kot* (digs) is a term the French-speakers have taken over from the Flemings. That the term is used on both sides of the language border is the result of the fact that French-speakers used to study at the University of Louvain until the time it was split. The University of Louvain was founded in 1425, which makes it one of the oldest in Europe. The town developed into a true university town. After the split in 1968 a new university town of Louvain-la-Neuve was created from nothing on the French-speaking side. The unusual architecture of the town is a good reflection of the spirit of the age in the early 1970s.

Chips

The unlimited opportunities for intimate contact with the other (or the same) sex is not the only thing parents worry about. There is also the menu. Many years of experience have taught that a liberated young Belgian eats too many chips. They eat *friet* (chips) from the *frietkot* (the chips shop), because it is quicker than cooking their own food, and in the university canteen they don't choose boiled potatoes or rice, but prefer the traditional fry-up of their native land.

University students in Louvain-la-Neuve, the university set up in 1968, when the French and Dutch speakers decided to go their separate ways.

What students have been doing for generations is the best experimental proof of something everyone knows already: if a Belgian has a choice, he chooses chips. The university is aware of this, too. It always makes sure that there is a plentiful supply of healthy food with lots of vegetables and fibre, vegetarian meals and meals acceptable to various religions, but it can't do much more than that. In Louvain, on the university's catering website, you will not only find the menu for the next few weeks but also good advice about food:

"ALMA (the University catering service) works hard to see that all the dishes on offer are balanced and to limit the amount of fat as much as possible. An ideal hot meal is one in which a maximum of 40 per cent of the energy is produced by fats".

"Yet it is mainly you yourself who decides how much fat you eat. Here is an example. If you eat a rumpsteak with baked beans, boiled potatoes and some gravy, that will give you 547 calories. 29 per cent of this energy comes from fats. If, however, you eat exactly the same meal, but with chips, then it works out at 884 calories (that is an increase of 337), and moreover, 44 per cent of the energy comes from fats. An enormous difference."

"Of course, you make your own choice, but that is the reason why at ALMA no dishes are offered to which chips are added beforehand. A crusade against chips? Absolutely not, our chips are in fact very tasty, but you should not have them too often."

Belgians love eating large quantities of chips.

In spite of all the health and diet crazes,
Belgians often still eat too much fat.

A Belgian Existence. Life As It Is

The weekly visit to the disco means a lot to many young people. In recent years there has been a great expansion of discos...

Sometimes, of course, students do their own cooking, but no one has any illusions about the variety of their diet: various thicknesses and shapes of pasta combined with various cheap brands of tomato sauce. Fortunately there are weekends. Then the students take home their dirty laundry and their mothers have the opportunity to fill a range of Tupperware containers with healthy food and give them good advice as well. Increasingly a microwave oven is becoming standard equipment in student digs.

"Serious" Entertainment Too

Belgium's young people also have their serious side. About 90 per cent go to cafés or pubs, and almost two-thirds of them dance themselves to a frazzle in discos, but it is not all dancing and drinking. About a third of young people between the ages of 16 and 25 also sometimes go to the theatre or the ballet. One in three buys concert tickets and one in two visits exhibitions and museums. Thirty per cent sometimes go to a public lecture, and 17 per cent do some kind of voluntary work. The cinema is very popular: almost nine out of ten young people go occasionally.

First Place In The EU

About six out of ten young people go on to higher education after secondary school, par-
ticularly the children of parents who did so themselves. Among young people whose
fathers actually have a degree, nine out of ten go on to higher education. Among those
whose fathers do not have a secondary diploma, less than half do so. 40 per cent of the
children of blue-collar workers go on to higher education. Children of people with a low
income are entitled to study grants.

All in all, Belgium has the highest number of 18 to 24-year olds in higher education:
32 per cent of Belgians in this age group are taking higher courses. That is more than in
any other EU country. The number of Belgians receiving a university degree each year is
steadily rising. Between 1987 and 1997 it grew by 18 per cent. In 1998, 9,993 men and
11,000 women obtained university degrees.

In Belgium there is a flourishing youth culture, in which music plays an important role. This does not only mean listening to pop music; many young people play their own compositions in groups.

Marriage is still a popular form of living together, in spite of the growing number of divorces.

88

Producing And Reproducing

Marrying And Staying Married... If Possible

Once studies are finally over, it is time to begin "real" life. That is to say, working for your keep and establishing some kind of family. "Man was not created to be alone," say bar room philosophers in Belgian cafés. Belgians marry later and divorce more easily than they used to. Also the days are gone when young people stayed at home with mum and dad until they had found "their true love" and married. Increasing numbers of young people live together for a while before they marry, or do not marry at all. Moreover, there are more and more intermediate arrangements such as "living apart together", and increasingly non-traditional forms of relationship are gaining official recognition. This does not mean that the traditional pattern is no longer followed. About eight out of ten Belgians still leave the parental home to plunge straight into marriage. For those who first live alone for a time, or live together with someone outside marriage, it is usually a question of deferment rather than renunciation. If they want children, or if one is on the way, many couples take the decision to marry, even though the acknowledgement of children born out of wedlock is not so difficult. The age at which two people, who were not previously married, marry each other is now on average 27 years and nine months for men and 25 years and seven months for women.

Celebrations

Once the starting signal has been given for a wedding, the couple and their parents rush into action. A date is agreed, and then the search begins for a hall where the party can be organised. This often has to be booked a year in advance. Belgians are very fond of holding their wedding receptions in castles, and with the highest castle density in the world, the problem is not so much to find a restaurant inside ancient walls, as to find a date one of them is free. Often the preparations for a wedding lead to friction as a result of differences of opinion. Should the couple marry in church or not, and what will Granny say if they don't? How many people should be invited, and who will pay for what? Will their darling daughter marry in white or not? Will it be formal dress with parents and grandparents and all the aunts and uncles in hired morning coats and long dresses at a grand reception, or will everything be limited to a new suit for the bridegroom and both fathers, and a new outfit for the ladies? The passions raised by these kinds of discussions can run surprisingly high.

Belgians like a stylish wedding in a
grand setting
© Oswald Pauwels

Hallelujah

A Belgian wedding involves first the civil marriage in the Town Hall, followed afterwards, if desired, by a ceremony in church.

Every Town Hall has its own particular style, but there is usually some provision for music. The quality of the music depends on the talent and enthusiasm of the official who has the job of providing the accompaniment to the ceremony. Once the marriage vows have been exchanged, they may be followed by a variety of musical pieces; Handel's Hallelujah Chorus is very popular. But more original choices are also possible. A reporter for a Dutch newspaper in Brussels was very pleasantly surprised when he married his Haitian love in a Brussels suburb. When everything had been said and signed, the loudspeakers burst into the Brabançonne, the Belgian national anthem. Everyone stood up and as the last note sounded began to sit down, when the Wilhelmus, the Dutch national anthem, started up. When that was over and everyone thought it was finished, along came the Haitian anthem. The couple and their family were very moved by the attention.

In recent years there has been a steady decline in church weddings. Around 49 per cent of couples still opt for a wedding in church. In 1967 that was 86 per cent. There are great differences between the three Regions: in Flanders 51 per cent still marry in church, in the Walloon Region 54 per cent, and in Brussels, where there are many foreign residents, only 20 per cent. In 1967, in the Metropolitan Region, 62 per cent still married in church.

"Just Another Scrap Of Paper"

The – we must assume – happy couple are given a "marriage book" by the burgomaster or the registrar. This contains their names and dates of birth, but that is not meant to be all. If the wedding is performed in church, the priest will add the details later in the day, and if all goes well, the names of their children will also be added later on. In the early 20th century there were still 24 lines provided for writing in the names of children, now there are fewer, but still enough to give people ideas. However, the subtle hint seems to be wasted on most couples. In spite of the glaring white spaces in their marriage books, Belgians are not producing enough children to maintain the population. For this the country would need a total fertility rate of 2.1 children per woman, but Belgium lies far below this with at 1.56.

Young couples also have to sign a marriage contract. They can have one drawn up by a lawyer or they can do nothing, in which case they fall under a system in which everything they bring into their marriage remains their personal property, but everything they acquire jointly in their marriage becomes property held in common.

There Are Other Ways

People who live together, whether or not they have a relationship, can if they wish sign a "cohabitation contract". They do so by submitting a document to the Town Hall in which they declare that they wish to live together legally. They then have rights and obligations to each other similar to those of a married couple. They can also have an agreement about property drawn up beforehand by a lawyer. The cohabitation contract is recorded in the population registers and is terminated only when one of the partners living together gets married or when one or both partners sign a declaration at the Town Hall that they wish to stop living together. The cohabitation contract was invented mainly as a result of pressure from the gay movement, which wanted to make their relationships official in this way and wanted to ensure that gay partners could inherit from each other. For gay couples, who want a religious form of ceremony, there is a non-official "liturgy of friendship".

Belgians still tend to choose monogamous relationships.

There Is Still (Some) Romance In The World

A survey of 4,000 Flemings shows what kind of relationships Belgians are looking for. They had to choose between "romantic love" (one love lasting a lifetime), a few "pure", exclusive relationships, or "polygamy" (a number of simultaneous relationships). The younger generations did not expect a relationship to last a lifetime, but among those over 50 the majority still held fast to the idea of a lifelong relationship.

	Romantic love	Pure relationships	Polygamy
Women	51%	46%	3%
Men	47%	47%	6%
16-19 years	25%	63%	12%
20-29 years	40%	54%	6%
30-39 years	40%	55%	5%
40-49 years	45%	49%	6%
50-59 years	53%	44%	3%
60-69 years	64%	32%	4%
+ 70 years	69%	29%	2%
no qualifications	67%	31%	2%
lower secondary	55%	42%	4%
higher secondary	45%	49%	5%
higher education	34%	59%	7%

What Type Relationship do they Prefer?　　　*Source: Panel survey of Belgian households*

Divorce: The Brief Pain

In spite of all good intentions at the outset, relationships and marriages sometimes run onto the rocks. Belgians are not in favour of needlessly prolonging the pain of people trapped in a bad marriage. In the opinion of present-day society divorce is an acceptable phenomenon, even though everyone thinks it is better avoided and practising Catholics are less quick to accept it than others. Yet the attitude of the Church to divorced people is quite understanding. After Great Britain, Belgium is the country where there are the most divorces. In 1995 there were 2.9 divorces per thousand population, compared with 3.5 in Great Britain. In the Netherlands the number of divorces per thousand population in 1995 was 2.2, in Germany 2.1, and in Sweden 2.6. France recorded two divorces per thousand population in 1994. 1995 was a peak year, because a new, more flexible, divorce law came into effect and a number of deferred divorces were applied for.

Divorce has become quite easy. In a divorce by mutual agreement the divorce procedure can be completed within six months. Couples who want a divorce make arrangements between themselves in advance about the division of property and bringing up children. They have to appear twice before a judge to confirm that they remain firm in their decision to end their marriage. The divorce can also be declared when a couple have in fact lived apart for two years and one of the partners requests it.

If there are children, they have the legal right to be heard in deciding the question of which parent they will live with. "Co-parenthood", in which the right of custody is granted to both parents, and the children spend part of their time with the father and part with the mother, is possible too. Grandparents and others who have a close link with the children also have an enforceable right of access.

	Marriages	Divorces	%
1990	38,257	10,610	27.7
1991	35,777	10,896	30.5
1992	34,412	11,610	33.7
1993	32,123	11,053	34.4
1994	30,681	11,542	37.7
1995	30,667	19,466	63.4
1996	30,228	14,684	48.5
1997	28,328	13,994	49.4
1998	25,631	13,973	54.5

Marriages and Divorces

Source: NIS

Work Ennobles

A familiar saying in Belgium is *Arbeid adelt* (Work ennobles), but that is not the first thing a working Belgian thinks of when he gets up in the morning. He thinks about the traffic he has to cope with. Belgians live on average 17 kilometres (10 miles) away from their work, so for 60 per cent of Belgians the working day starts by climbing behind the steering wheel of a car. About 9 per cent are driven to work as passengers.

Commuters in Brussels Central Station. The train is an efficient and ecologically responsible means of transport.

In the morning a great deal of this commuter traffic goes into Brussels. Some 222,000 Flemings work there. From the Walloon Region about 116,000 commute each day into the capital of Belgium and Europe. About 24,000 Flemings work in Walloon areas, while 32,000 Walloons earn

their living in Flanders. The number of Brussels residents working in Flanders amounts to 28,000 and another 14,000 work in the Walloon Region. Of the Flemings 89 per cent work in their own region, for the Walloons this figure is 85 per cent, and for the residents of Brussels 83 per cent.

As in most countries, this toing and froing leads to traffic queues. The ring road round Brussels is particularly notorious. The stress induced by the traffic brings everyone's worst characteristics to the surface, in Belgium as much as anywhere else. About half the drivers of company cars, in other words, people who do a great deal of driving for their work, admit to driving aggressively. A quarter say that they have felt threatened in traffic. Eight out of ten do not obey the speed limit. This kind of driver claims to waste about two hours and 18 minutes every week in traffic jams.

Like their fellow sufferers elsewhere, Belgians place their hopes in teleworking to be rescued from this commuting misery. However, teleworking is still in the infant stage. In Belgium 5.3 per cent of employees work all or some of the time at home. In this respect the country is in seventh place in the EU.

Simply The Best

If you see him in traffic you would not believe it, but once a Belgian gets to work, he is a good and disciplined member of the workforce. Perhaps, indeed, the best in the world. In every international comparison Belgian employees come out shining. They are always on the winners' stand, if not with the gold medal, then with silver or bronze.

Take productivity. International comparisons of productivity show that the average Belgian is the most productive worker in the world per working hour. And if you look at productivity per year, Belgians again score very high. According to data from the International Labour Organisation, the average Belgian employee in 1997 produced an added value of US$ 49,187 per year, and only had to yield to his American counterpart, who led with US$ 49,905. The rest of the world follows well behind. Third was the average Irish employee at US$ 44,253.

Daily queues confront Belgians with
an ever-growing traffic problem.
© Paul De Malsche

The Belgian And His Work

Nothing is so pitiful as a man in a made-to-measure suit, opening his briefcase, slipping his hand in, pulling out his packed lunch, and without even glancing at it, throwing it into the waste-bin.

Nevertheless, this kind of deposit is an everyday occurrence in Belgium. Every morning, spouses lovingly make sandwiches of cheese and jam. Every afternoon the discarded packages mark their affection in aluminium foil, indicating the spots where, for the Belgian, the dividing line between home and work is to be found: on the train, at the station, at the tram stop, mostly in a rubbish-bin. Belgians do not like to take their work home, nor do they like taking home with them to work. They are resolute about it. In the workplace a very different style of conviviality prevails. They call it "the working atmosphere". And no hormonal eruption of devotedly buttered sandwiches could ever be a match for the "atmosphere at work". Not even higher pay will weigh against the importance of that "working atmosphere". Belgians are prepared to do anything to keep their working atmosphere as pleasant as possible. Having lunch together in a nearby café. Playing football together. Collecting stamps together. Playing the Lottery together. Buying a sandwich together. Just as long as it is together. Only the moaners and the misers bring sandwiches from home.

"These are sobering results," was a specialist in personnel management's comment on a study examining the Belgian's perception of his work. The investigation Working Today clearly revealed that Belgian employees regarded the atmosphere at work as the most important factor in their job. "What factor makes your work attractive?", the Belgian was asked. "A good working atmosphere," was clearly equally rated, and sometimes scored even better, than "an exciting job with a future" or "job security". Slightly more than 60 per cent of Belgians, another study revealed, said they enjoyed themselves at work. Laurette Onkelinx, Minister of Employment, is aware of it, too. No proof is required that some enjoy themselves at the expense of others. Which explains why she has a number of bills at the ready to prevent harassment in the workplace. It will benefit our economy.

The better the working atmosphere, the more loyal the Belgian will be to his boss. The study also revealed that sixty60 per cent of Belgians consider the economy favourable for looking for a job. Nevertheless, most of them will stay in the familiar work surroundings they have known for many years. For those employees with between three and ten years' experience, not one in four had applied for a job in the last three years. Job-hopping is really not the Belgians' cup of tea. A sauna at work, neck massage in the office, is not necessary either. Work is work and home is home. Which explains the sandwich mountain.

Anna Luyten
Journalist with the daily De Standaard.

As far as quality is concerned, the Belgian is a highflier. According to the Global Labour Force Evaluation Report the quality of the Belgian workforce, after those of Singapore and Switzerland, is the highest in the world. The Beri Research Bureau surveys employees in 49 industrialised countries. They look at wage rates, productivity, technical skills, the attitude of workers, absenteeism rates and the costs of employee participation and labour legislation.

Belgium scored 73 out of a possible 100. This puts it equal to Japan and above countries such as the United States (70), France (66) and Germany (63). After the Japanese, the Belgian is also the most reliable worker. He does not stay at home without a reason. Belgium has the lowest absenteeism rate in the EU. Of course, his linguistic ability is also a plus for the Belgian employee. For foreign businesses the quality of the workforce is one of the most important reasons why they come to Belgium. Almost half a million Belgians work for foreign companies.

World Champion Car Builder

The high productivity of Belgian employees is also the reason why the country has attracted so many car assembly plants. Since the 1930s and the disappearance of the legendary Minerva, "the car of maharajahs and film stars", Belgians have no car marques of their own. They assemble foreign cars. Ford, Volvo, Opel and Volkswagen all have assembly plants in Belgium. In 2000 these plants together produced more than 1 million cars. If you look at production per head of population, Belgium is the largest car producer in the world.

Of all Europeans, the Belgians are the keenest car assemblers.
© Volvo/Johan Marten

Just Deserts

Of course, people want to be paid for hard work and preferably as much as possible. And just like anywhere else, everyone in Belgium thinks that they are underpaid for everything they do for their boss. The boss himself, it goes without saying, thinks he pays too much. To some extent both parties are right. In comparison with other countries employees get their hands on very little of the gross wage paid by the boss. The difference goes to the state, and among other things pays for the social security system. Since there has been rather more flexibility in the finances of the Belgian state, social security contributions by employers have gradually been reduced and labour costs have come down.

	Brussels Metropolitan Region	Flemish Region	Walloon Region	Total
(NACE C-K, full-time employees)	2,032	2,341	1,977	1,932
Occupation				
Management and executive	3,803	4,003	3,722	3,609
Professional and academic	2,743	2,819	2,708	2,726
Professional and academic-related	2,297	2,382	2,298	2,210
Clerical	1,940	2,018	1,938	1,829
Service and sales staff	1,542	1,605	1,532	1,520
Tradesmen and skilled workers	1,699	1,806	1,684	1,694
Factory workers, machine operators and assembly-line workers	1,756	1,743	1,756	1,757
Unskilled workers	1,568	1,523	1,587	1,527
Industry (NACE)				
Extractive industries (NACE C)	1,843		1,960	1,822
Manufacturing (NACE D)	2,013	2,156	2,009	1,983
Utilities (NACE E)	2,852	3,328	2,772	2,674
Construction (NACE F)	1,779	1,915	1,775	1,722
Wholesale and retail trade; repair of cars and domestic appliances (NACE G)	1,902	2,295	1,810	1,743
Hotels en restaurants (NACE H)	1,526	1,689	1,461	1,422
Transport, storage and communication (NACE I)	1,939	2,035	1,952	1,828
Financial services (NACE J)	2,617	2,677	2,491	2,693
Real estate, rentals and services to businesses (NACE K)	2,265	2,478	2,136	2,148

Gross Monthly Pay (€) by Occupation and Industry (October 1995)

Source: NIS, Inquiry into the structure and distribution of salaries (1995).

Linking wages to the index ensures that Belgians keep their purchasing power.

On the whole there are few conflicts over wages in Belgium. That can be ascribed to the very specific system of collective bargaining and the fact that wages are still automatically linked to the Consumer Price Index. This index-linking has great symbolic significance for Belgians and whenever anyone suggests it should be abolished, they come up against enormous opposition. It has been the subject of frequent discussions which up to now have been won by those who think that the system has more advantages than disadvantages. Collective wage negotiations are more transparent if adjustments for inflation do not have to be negotiated at the same time. And if there is no automatic wage adjustment, wage negotiations are always accompanied by demands based on an estimate of future inflation, which is usually overestimated, say the supporters of the existing system. The system also contributes a great deal to social peace. Belgium is, in comparison with other countries, a country with very few strikes.

Of course Belgians are not naive. They are aware of the weak points of the system. They have learnt from the 1970s, when inflation shot up dizzyingly as a result of the high price of oil, and therefore wages, too, were forced up. So a typically Belgian compromise was found: wages are now linked to the "health index". In calculating this index oil products and tobacco products are not included. This index rises less rapidly than the "old" one.

When a few years back it was decided to keep automatic index-linking, a number of limitations were also agreed to prevent Belgian wages rising faster than in neighbouring countries. In any case, in Belgium the growth of wages is closely watched, so that the competitive position of the country is not weakened. Belgium has a "law on competitive strength" and every two years trade unions, the government and employers jointly determine the "wage norm", i.e. the maximum percentage by which wages may rise in the next two years. In doing so they look at productivity and the situation in other countries.

Apart from that more and more Belgians are not rewarded by wages alone. Alternative forms of remuneration, such as stock options, profit sharing and supplementary pensions are increasingly being introduced.

Bosses And Staff Need Not Be Adversaries

Belgium is a country with a consultative economy. Everything to do with work is regulated by "collective bargaining": in other words, by agreements between the organs representing the employers and the employees, the "social partners". The government plays a mediating role, or breaks the impasse if the other two parties can't come to an agreement.

Belgium is a country with a corporative economy. Everything to do with work is arranged by collective bargaining.

The basis for this system was laid down during the Second World War. Employers and employees moved closer to each other as a consequence of the Occupation. Often they conspired toge-

ther in sabotaging production, or bosses lost or falsified records of their employees to protect them from forced labour in Germany. On 19 August 1944, still before the Liberation, trade unions and employers signed the "Draft Agreement for Social Solidarity", incorporating the principles on which their mutual relationship would be based. This came down to the employees acknowledging the authority of their boss and promising to do their work well, and the employers binding themselves to respect the dignity of their employees and treat them fairly. They also recognised the right of employees to organise themselves. In addition the document contains a description of a social security system. A law on social security for employees was signed as early as 28 December 1944, the day the Battle of the Ardennes ended. In 1956 representatives of trade unions and employers signed the "Productivity Declaration", in which employers accepted the principle that the wages of employees should rise as productivity increases.

Since the war the principle of consultation has gradually been expanded. In practice, there is a continuous dialogue at various levels between the representatives of employees and employers. There is consultation at the company level, at the level of industries, and at the national level. At the company level the interests of the employees are looked after by the Works Council, the Committee for Health and Safety at Work and the recognition of trade unions. At the industry level there are joint industrial committees. Employers, employees and representatives of government can make agreements about wages and terms of employment and confirm these by signing collective labour agreements (CAOs). These can be concluded at the level of the firm or at the national level. Nationally the Central Council for Trade and Industry (Centrale Raad voor het Bedrijfsleven – CRB) and the National Council for Labour (Nationale Arbeidsraad – NAR) are the consultation bodies. The CRB advises the government. The NAR has real authority to negotiate. This is where CAOs and "central agreements" are reached, applying to all businesses throughout the country. Collective bargaining is one of the most productive makers of compromises in the Belgian tradition.

Six Out Of Ten In A Trade Union

The consultation model could not exist if there were no trade unions. There are three trade union federations in Belgium: the Christian Trade Union Federation (Algemeen Christelijk Vakverbond – ACV), the socialist Belgian Trade Union Federation (Algemeen Belgisch Vakverbond – ABVV), and the Federation of Liberal Trade Unions (Algemene Centrale der Liberale Vakverbonden – ACLVB). If they act jointly they are referred to as the "Common Trade Union Front". After the Scandinavian countries Belgium has the highest degree of trade union membership in the world. Sixty per cent of employees are members of a trade union.

Money Must Circulate

What a Belgian does with his money says much about his prosperity. Just a small part of his income provides him with enough to eat. Most of his money is spent on his house and his car.

Categories	1999
Food, drink and tobacco	15.8%
Clothing and shoes	5.3%
Gross rent	21.2%
Heating, light and water	4.9%
Furniture and domestic appliances	6.5%
Health	4.7%
Transport and communication	14.5%
Culture and recreation	9.0%
Hotels/restaurants	5.0%
Tourism	3.1%
Financial services and insurance	4.8%
Other expenses	5.2%

Family Expenditure as a Percentage of Family Income

Source: NIS

Renting is for most Belgians a transitional stage, something they do when they are young. As soon as they have saved enough, they go to the bank and the architect. When these have reduced their dreams and wishes to a realistic project, the builder can be set to work and the adrenaline begins to flow. Builders never start when they promised to, and always do something that gives the owner sufficient material to complain about for the rest of his life. People who can't stand women who always talk about their labour pains in great detail should certainly avoid conversations where the word "building" crops up. A list of horror stories about walls out of true, the wrong kind of layout, "cowboy" builders, lazy joiners, expensive electricians and incompetent architects, once it started only stops when someone says: "Yes, people ought really to have two goes at building a house." Which again proves that Belgians are a strange people. They think building is a nightmare, but can't stop doing it.

The houses they build are always the most individual expression of the most individual taste. Every house is different and that, of course, has consequences for the neighbourhood. Belgian streets are always the scene of clashes between different styles and architectural ambitions. However, no one feels themselves called upon to do anything drastic about this happy form of anarchy and everyone goes cheerfully ahead with the realisation of their dreams.

Belgians are born with an urge to build. Owning their house – preferably with a garden – is far more popular than renting.

The Belgian's reputation is assured, as it rests on solid foundations: more than 60 per cent of the Belgians own their own home. Brussels is the only exception to this, where the proportion of 60 per cent tenants is pretty much the opposite. The brick in the stomach: it is a reality.

Although the size of the average family has become smaller (from 4.3 members at the beginning of the 20th century to 2.4 at the end of the same century) the number of dwellings has risen appreciably (from 1.8 million to 4.3 million in the same period). It seems that each occupant needs increasingly more space. The Belgian makes things easy for himself in his house or flat and makes a considerable investment in his nest: the portion of the budget dedicated to the home has doubled from 14 to 28 per cent in the period mentioned.

Naturally, the construction sector is rather inflated by this national inclination. There was actually a slump in the 1980s but afterwards the brick made its presence felt once again. In 2000 the building of more than 42,000 homes was started.

During the final years of the millennium, renovation came into its own: in 2000 more than 26,500 renovation projects were undertaken. The Belgian sands down, scours out, rediscovers the warmth of wood, swears allegiance to all things "bio", arranges and re-arranges the home in function of every change in the family composition. The Flemings especially went wild about renovation. Hardly surprising, when the more stringent town planning regulations ensured that the remaining building plots came in short supply. And although purchasing power might be greater in Flanders than in Wallonia, people were very apprehensive about the purchase of such land because of speculation. In contrast, in Wallonia building continued apace. There the administrative restrictions are not (yet) so stringent and the economic recovery is coupled to a government campaign in support of the entire housing sector.

In Brussels, the target of all European desires, the arrival of European functionaries and the economic activity sucked along in their wake, has led to the renovation of entire districts. The money is there and so is the interest. Eurocrats like old houses with high ceilings, decorations from the beginning of the century and beautiful Art Nouveau rooms. The Brussels lifestyle combines high-quality comfort with the restoration of existing buildings and that is rather different from the period between 1970 and 1990, the crazy years of thoughtless demolition. Also in the so-called immigrant neighbourhoods, new Belgians are investing in bricks and mortar for the family. Whatever is said of them, these people have their roots in a history and lifestyle which is in common with ours. The most prosperous Brussels inhabi-

tants, both indigenous and immigrant, are rediscovering the beauty of Art Deco flats and, as a result, of communal possession, because it often concerns impressively large dwellings. In short, the home has once more become a valuable refuge and investment whilst simultaneously providing an appropriate backdrop for that certain savoir-vivre. Once more there is work in the building sector, even if working unofficially or 'in the black' remains a wides-

pread phenomenon of unknown proportions – and this last fact has its reasons for existence. The building industry will be based on sound foundations in the new millennium and can look forward to an assured future – not a virtual one!

Gabrielle Lefèvre

Journalist with the daily Le Soir.

Always On Sunday

Once his brick cocoon is in position, the Belgian fills it with furniture. In many cases Ikea will have a hand in this, as that chain is the leader in the Belgian furniture market. Two out of three Belgian families have an Ikea catalogue in their home. For those who do not like Ikea, there is still Sunday. Belgium is strewn with great furniture temples which enjoy an exemption from the laws on opening hours, and are allowed to open on Sundays. For several years looking at furniture has been a popular pastime with which many Belgian families fill their Sundays. In the big furniture stores, where you can always get something to eat and drink, you can also find many middle-aged Belgians. Once the children are out of the house, and the house itself is paid off, parents think that they can indulge themselves a little. "Refurbishing" is part of it.

Belgian houses usually have a garden too, so more than 62 per cent of Belgians at times have to take their lawnmower out of the garage. About 2.7 per cent of Belgians have a second home in Belgium, and 0.8 per cent have one abroad.

We Do The Washing Up Ourselves

When it comes to comfort at home, most Belgians are well provided for. As many as 97 per cent have a colour television and nine out of ten families are connected to cable television, so they have a choice of dozens of channels, in various languages. In spite of this availability Belgian families continually moan that "there is nothing on TV". Fortunately there is always the video recorder. Seven out of ten Belgians have one. It has been calculated that the average Belgian, firmly ensconced on his sofa, so carefully chosen on Sunday, spends 8.5 years of his life watching TV. If he does not watch TV, he listens to music. One or more hi-fi installations can be found in seven out of ten Belgian houses.

Those who think that some programmes on TV are more boring than watching the washing machine, have not far to go. In nine out of ten families there is a washing machine with an attractive selection of programmes.

A surprising phenomenon in Belgian houses, which are usually filled with every conceivable appliance, is the relative absence of dishwashers. In more than 60 per cent of families the washing up is still done by hand. Perhaps this has something to do with the adage: "If you want it done properly, do it yourself."

My Car, My Freedom

From the proportion of his income devoted to it, it is plain to see that the Belgian is attached to his motorcar. There are 4 million families in Belgian and 4.4 million cars. One family in five has no car, and one family in five has more than one. More than 5 per cent of families travel in a company car and 0.8 per cent have two cars paid for by the boss. The most frequently purchased car in 2000 was the VW Golf, followed by the Opel Astra, Renault Mégane, VW Polo and Opel Corsa.

A Man Must Eat

The Belgian diet has changed. Many Belgians nowadays skip breakfast, so that consumption of bread is much reduced.

Belgians have a good appetite but not such a healthy one. One in three Belgians skips breakfast. As a result, consumption of bread is much reduced from what it used to be. Fifty years ago

The national sport is beer-drinking.

the average Belgian still ate 137 kilos of bread a year, now it is only 53 kilos. On average Belgians consume three tablespoonfuls of vegetables per day, half the amount recommended by nutrition specialists. Of all Europeans, Belgians eat the most fat. According to the National Nutrition Council their eating habits lie at the basis of 65 per cent of the causes of death. Belgians drink less beer than they used to, but still put away a good quantity: 104 litres per year per head of population. Lager is the great favourite, followed by amber beer, white beer and the heavy Trappist and Abbey beers. Technically these last two are the same, but according to Belgian law only beers brewed within abbey walls can bear the name 'Trappist'. The same beers brewed outside must be labelled "Abbey beers".

Belgians Love France

An important item of expense for Belgian families is travel. Belgians lead the EU in expenditure on holidays and recreation. When the bravest of the Gauls go on holiday, their first choice is France. Spain and the Netherlands take second and third place in the hierarchy of favourite holiday destinations. Then follow Italy, Germany, Austria, the United Kingdom, Switzerland, Greece and Turkey.

A Sound Safety Net

If you are ill or out of work you are well protected in Belgium. If the country has about the lowest degree of poverty in the world, that, say the experts, is the consequence of efficient social security. With its social security Belgium succeeds in keeping 80 per cent of those who would, without help, be poor, out of the poverty statistics. This means that it has, together with Sweden, the most effective social security system in the world.

Social security is financed about 80 per cent by the contributions of employees and employers (a fixed percentage of gross wages), about 18 per cent by the state, and the rest by income from other sources.

Unemployment Allowances

To enjoy unemployment benefits, the unemployed person must have worked a certain number of days, and paid his contributions. The number of days necessary depends on the person's age. Only those unemployed who have lost their job through no fault of their own, qualify for unemployment benefits. Others will have to apply to the OCMW (Public Centre for Social Relief) to have an income at all..

Those with a family to support receive 60 per cent of their wage for the whole period of their unemployment, subject to a maximum limit of BEF 60,000 (EUR 1,487) gross. Single people receive 60 per cent for the first year, and 40 per cent thereafter. An unemployed person living with someone but with no children to support gets 55 per cent for the first year, 35 per cent for the next three months, and thereafter a lump sum of BEF 522 (EUR 12.94) or BEF 696 (EUR 17.25) per day. A person living with someone else, with no family to support and not making enough effort to find work, may lose his entitlement through prolonged unemployment. This does not apply to those over 50, or to the unemployed whose total family income would fall below a certain minimum if they lost their benefits.

Subsistence Level

For those who come under no other system, there is the "subsistence level". That pays BEF 29,000 (EUR 719) for spouses living together or those who have a minor child living with them. Single people must get by on BEF 21,700 (EUR 538). To get subsistence level payments they have to register with the OCMW.

Health Insurance

In sickness the allowance depends on the employee's status. For blue-collar workers a different system applies than for office workers. For the first two weeks blue-collar workers are paid their full normal wage. The following week they get 86 per cent of their wage, the subsequent two weeks they drop to 60 per cent with a maximum of BEF 2,263 (EUR 56) per day. For heads of families and single persons this continues, for those living with someone the percentage drops to 55 per cent. For office workers the rule is that they receive their full salary for the first month, after which the same rules apply as for blue-collar workers. Government employees come under a special system. They are entitled to their full wage for 21 working days. After that it depends on their length of service. For every year they have worked they are entitled to one month's "sick leave" with full pay. This "credit" can be accumulated. If a government employee is ill for so long that it is used up, he drops to 60 per cent of his pay.

Four Weeks Of Holiday

The annual holiday entitlement is calculated from the number of days worked in the previous year. It amounts to two days paid holiday for every month worked. In addition to that there is a supplement, "holiday money", amounting to three weeks and two days pay. Additional entitlements or holiday money beyond the legal requirements can be agreed within individual companies.

Family Allowances

The family allowance paid to employees amounts to BEF 2,816 (EUR 69.8) for the first child, BEF 5,210 (EUR 129.2) for the second, and BEF 7,778 (EUR 192.8) for each child after that. These sums increase with the age of the child.

Maternity Leave

Expectant mothers are entitled to 14 weeks pre- and postnatal leave. For the first month they receive 82 per cent of their pay, with no limit. After that they get 75 per cent, but subject to a maximum limit. They are also entitled to a maternity allowance of BEF 38,141 (EUR 945) for the first child and BEF 28,697 (EUR 711.4) for additional children.

Pensions

Pensions depend on the career, the wage and the family circumstances of the pensioner. Those with a full working career behind them can count on at least BEF 38,000 (EUR 942) per month for a couple. Single people are entitled to a minimum of BEF 30,000 (EUR 744). For those who do not qualify for some form of pension because they have never worked, there is a guaranteed income. It comes to BEF 30,000 (EUR 744) for couples and BEF 22,800 (EUR 565) for single people.

Belgians are long-lived. Life expectation for men is seventy-five, for women on average eighty-one.

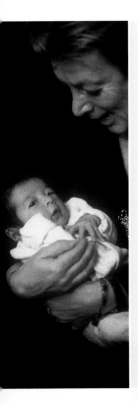

No Waiting Lists

75 per cent of the cost of ordinary general health care is reimbursed. If you land in hospital you need not pay as long as you are satisfied with a general ward, although anyone who wants a private room, or a two-bedded one, must pay for it. But a small sum will have to be paid for nursing care and medicines. Many people have private hospital insurance to which their employer contributes a part.

For medication an "excess" must be paid. That is a specific percentage of the price, subject to a certain maximum. It depends on the kind of treatment. Nothing has to be paid for life-saving medicines. For other very useful medication the patients may have to pay 20 per cent of the cost themselves, and so on.

Belgians have a tendency to use a lot of medicines and are very ready to ring up the doctor. Nor do they normally have to wait long for an operation. In contrast to the situation in some other countries, there are no waiting lists.

Winding Down

The official retirement age is still 65, but few Belgians work that long. Only one in three work after they are 50. There are 1.8 million people in the 50 to 65 age group. Of these only 600,000 still work. A quarter of them are self-employed.

Among the no longer active are the 50,000 people who have taken early retirement, mainly with "bridging pensions" (a pension formula by which people get unemployment benefits supplemented by a fixed sum paid by their last employer). In addition are the 150,000 unemployed who are no longer obliged to look for work because they are over 50. There are also 300,000 who can take early retirement before they are 65 because they are in a special category. This includes, for instance, railway workers, police, the armed services and teachers. There are also another 300,000 Belgians, all women, who do not work and enjoy no benefits.

What can be a very attractive situation for the individual Belgian, is in fact a problem for the country as a whole. All these inactive people means that in this age group Belgium only has an employment rate of 36 per cent, far below the European average of 48 per cent. The expense of all these Belgians who have dropped out early runs high, and when added to those already on a pension it becomes steadily more difficult for those in work to bear the burden.

Preparation For The "Granddad Boom"

Like other countries, Belgium is preparing for the extra expense when the Baby-Boom generation retires. As this generation gets older, so the expenditure on medical care will also increase. Currently Belgium pays out 9.4 per cent of its GNP on pensions and 6.2 per cent on health care. By the year 2040 that may have gone up to 13 per cent and 9.2 per cent respectively. The government is trying to deal with this problem by building up a budgetary reserve, the "Silver Fund."

What the Belgian Pensioner Does With His Time

Sometimes it seems as if Belgians spend a lifetime "growing" toward their retirement. They hanker after it, like good schoolchildren long for prize-giving day and the long summer holidays that follow. That is exactly what the Belgian is striving for: a retirement with plenty of time to himself. To cast off the years of hard work. While governments all over Europe are threatening to keep their subjects at the treadmill right up to 70, the Belgians want to retire earlier and earlier. At 55 if they have to, but at 50 if at all possible.

It is a remarkable phenomenon. Belgians have been able to win the reputation of being hard workers — you might call them "workaholics". They like to be called that. But it is just as true that they want to cast off their work addiction as early as possible. And then the road to retirement lies before them. That is enough for the former workaholic to burst into bloom. A thousand new skills sprout from the branches of his imagination. He will swap two left hands for two right hands. He will mend his leaking roof, dig a flood drain for rain-water, construct a water fountain in his garden, build a carport or a superfluous summerhouse with materials that he has been putting aside for the last five years with an eye to the retirement of his dreams. And in his spare time he will fix things for his children. In his "spare" time. But that gets scarcer every day. Because there are also evening classes in Spanish. And cycle rides. And railway trips. All of them things that have got to be done.

Since the time that train travel was made virtually free for Belgian senior citizens, you can't keep them off the trains. Day in, day out they travel around their little country, backwards and forwards, to and fro. From the northern heaths to the Walloon Black Country, from the seaside resorts to the eastern heights. They nestle comfortably in their cheap train seats and migrate like swallows on their way south.

Young people on the way to school or work often can't find a seat and then look at them with envy.

When the sun shines, pensioners descend on café terraces rather like their beloved pigeons do on town squares. They drink ice cold beer in the shadow of the parasols. And there is always a carillon somewhere near, tunefully ticking off the hours of the twilight of their lives. Contentedly they sit breathing in the exhaust gases of the tourist buses which pollute the buildings and their lungs. Sitting outside cafés is probably the most popular sport for them. And then there is watching football and cycle races. Senior citizins love sport in their own way. They leave it to footballers to kick the ball about, they let the cyclists pedal, they let the pigeons fly. As pensioners they cannot do it all themselves any more. So they sit in front of the cafés – listed Belgians in front of listed buildings. Pensioners who, one and all, were born Ancient Belgians.

Miel Dekeyzer
Former radio journalist for Flemish radio and Television (VRT)

Many pensioners still lead a very active life.

Life's Twilight Years The Belgian Way
A Long Life

Life leads to death, and that profundity applies to Belgians too. By the time they finally leave it, most of them have a long life behind them, most of which they enjoyed in good health.

The average life expectancy is around 75 years for men and 81 for women. Flemings live longer than Walloons or people from Brussels. If you are born a woman in Flanders you hold the best hand.

	men	women
Brussels Metropolitan Region	74.75	80.96
Flemish Region	75.76	81.62
Walloon Region	73.15	80.16
Belgium	74.81	81.08

Life Expectancy at Birth in 1998 (years) *Source: NIS*

A Belgian Existence. Life As It Is

For those who have meanwhile reached the blessed age of 60, the figures are even more favourable. Men who are now 60 can expect to add another 19 years to it, and women at this age have on average another 24 years to their credit. These can well be interesting years, since there is a good chance that they will be reasonably healthy. Until they are 75, a majority of old people feel well or indeed very well.

Age group	Good or very good	Very bad to reasonable
15 to 24 years	91.1%	8.9%
25 to 34 years	90.0%	10.0%
35 to 44 years	79.6%	20.4%
45 to 54 years	77.0%	23.0%
55 to 64 years	67.5%	32.5%
65 to 74 years	56.3%	43.7%
75 years and over	45.3%	54.7%

Subjective Perception of State of Health (1997)

Source: 1997 Health survey conducted by the Wetenschappelijk Instituut Volksgezondheid (Louis Pasteur), in conjunction with the NIS and the Limburgs Universitair Centrum

Getting older does not necessarily mean that Belgians sit slumped in front of their TVs. A high proportion of elderly Belgians are still active outdoors. Between the ages of 65 and 75 almost one in ten goes occasionally to the cinema, and among those over 75 some still see a film. Theatre is even more popular. 12 per cent of the elderly between 65 and 75 occasionally go to the theatre and among those who have passed the peak of 75, the figure is still 5 per cent. One in five of those over 65 sometimes goes to a concert, and among those over 75 there is still one in every 20 who goes out for a dose of good music. Exhibitions and museums also attract them: in the age group from 66 to 75 one in three sometimes visits them, and among those over 75 still one in every 20.

Visiting cafés or pubs is of course the chief recreation. Even among those over 75 a third still sometimes go out for a pint. About 15 per cent of this age group claim that one is never too old to learn and go to lectures. Half of them are members of some club or other and one in ten do volunteer work.

Help? No Thank You

Some Very Ancient Belgians are still quite capable of looking after themselves. Two out of three of those over 80 still live in their own homes and can normally look after themselves without home nursing. Of the approximately 400,000 over-80s in Belgium, about 75,000 live in a home. Some 60,000 of them in an ordinary nursing home, the rest need so much extra care that they are accommodated in a home where special intensive nursing is available. One in seven over-80s (55,000) get regular care in their own homes.

Of course, the need for extra care increases with age. Among the 50,000 Belgians over 90, about one in five calls on home nursing, 30 per cent are in nursing homes, and about 8 per cent in homes with more intensive care.

In most cases Belgians choose to be buried, but the number of cremations is increasing.

As The End Approaches

Cause of death (absolute numbers)	1992	1993	1994	1995
Aids	149	172	193	221
Suicide	1,878	2,142	2,131	2,155
Cancer	27,489	27,955	27,971	28,350
Lung cancer and related diseases	6,596	6,679	6,578	6,777
Cancer of the digestive system	7,332	7,530	7,613	7,563
Skin cancer	293	264	282	243
Breast cancer	2,364	2,398	2,567	2,585
Prostate cancer	1,713	1,813	1,814	1,846
Stomach cancer	1,335	1,310	1,255	1,183
Cancer of the colon	2,376	2,339	2,594	2,468
Brain tumour	759	723	763	826
Cardiovascular diseases	38,499	40,391	38,780	39,076
Heart attack	7,773	8,926	8,294	8,372
Traffic accident	1,623	1,704	1,815	1,592
Accidental fall	1,305	1,420	1,430	1,252
Accident caused by fire	103	81	116	110
Murder	168	201	184	169

Cause of Death - Absolute Numbers (1992-1995)

Source: NIS

Cardiovascular diseases are responsible for more than half the mortality. Cancer is the second cause of death. Men are more likely to die of cancer than women. In 1994, 30.8 per cent of male deaths could be ascribed to cancer compared to 23.1 per cent of female deaths. Cardiovascular diseases were the cause of 41.5 per cent of female deaths, and 33.3 per cent of male deaths.

Talking About Dying

Recently there was a change in official medical ethics in Belgium. Doctors are now obliged to tell patients if they are dying. The doctor may only be silent if the patient does not want to know how serious his condition is, or if telling him would aggravate his condition. In the past it was different. The rule then was that a fatal prognosis should only exceptionally be divulged and with great circumspection. The change is the result of the debate about euthanasia. In practice many doctors were already following a policy of greater openness.

Dying With Dignity

In Belgium, too, the discussion about dying with dignity is in full swing. For many years there has been pressure for a law on euthanasia. There is a bill going through parliament at the moment, supported by the government parties; the Christian Democratic opposition parties are against it. Euthanasia has in any case long been quietly practised. There is also an association of supporters of euthanasia, which has adopted the name "The Right to Die with Dignity". This association has also recently been promoting the wider use of the "living will", a declaration in which someone lets it be known in advance that they want their life to be terminated if it no longer responds to a certain quality at the physical or spiritual level. These wills would forestall the possibility of people not being able to make their wishes known because of their physical state.

The opponents of the legalisation of euthanasia press for the further development of the possibilities of palliative care. There are centres where terminally ill patients can be cared for until their death and there are departments in hospitals specially reserved for these patients. There are also associations dedicated to the care of such patients in their own homes. These are subsidised by the state and by the Regions. Recently terminally ill patients who receive palliative care at home

121

have become entitled to a subsidy of BEF 19,500 (EUR 493) per month, for a maximum of two months, to help pay certain expenses. The family or friends of terminally ill patients are entitled to a career break for palliative care for a maximum of two months to look after a sick relative. Apart from that, employees are entitled to a 12-month career break for the care or psychological support of members of their family or relatives up to the second degree. During this "palliative leave" or career break to look after a relative, the carers are given an allowance of around BEF 20,000 (EUR 496) per month.

A Quick Last Visit To The Church

Most Belgians still choose a church ceremony as a farewell ritual, though here, too, the crumbling away of the religious sector's "market share" is plainly evident.

Church funeral	1967	1973	1980	1990	1998
Belgium	84.3	84.3	83.0	81.4	76.6
Flanders	91.3	91.3	90.7	88.8	83.6
Walloon provinces	79.3	80.0	78.2	76.8	73.6
Brussels	72.0	68.4	64.2	60.4	48.7

Percentage of Church Funerals

Source: 'Verloren zekerheid' by K. Dobbelaere, M. Elchardus, J. Kerkhofs and L. Voyé

In most cases the choice is still for burial, but the number of cremations increases year by year. Between 1984 and 1999 it trebled to 33,800, which amounts to one in every three deaths. And in two cases out of three the ashes are scattered. Traditionally funerals end with a reception. Usually this is confined to the immediate family, but there have been cases where the reception involved several hundred people. Those who are expected at the reception receive an invitation with the announcement of the death. In some regions the reception does not stop at coffee and rolls, with a pint afterwards, but those who attended the burial are confronted with a full cooked meal preceded by an aperitif and ending with coffee and liqueurs, with all kinds of interesting things in between.

Everyone A Donor

In Belgium in theory everyone is an organ donor. Only if someone has expressed his oppo-sition in writing during his life, or if his family do so after his death, are the doctors not allo-wed to remove any organs. Those who want to prevent their organs from being removed after death must make a declaration to this effect at their town hall. They are then given a card to carry on their person. Some 190,000 Belgians have made use of this right. Conversely, those who want to prevent their family objecting to their organs being removed can also make a declaration at their town hall. They are then given a donor card. Some 24,000 Belgians have taken the trouble to take this extra precaution. After their death even objection by their family cannot prevent their organs being removed. Nowadays doctors who discuss the removal of organs with the relatives of the deceased, still come up against refusals in about 15 per cent of cases.

Inheriting

Death implies inheritances. The aversion of Belgians to paying taxes is never so great as when inheritance is involved. Belgians do not find it logical that the state should take away yet more of the money for which their parents worked so hard and on which taxes have already been paid. The ingenuity with which inheritance taxes are avoided is consequently very great and books about "inheritance planning" are very popular.

Inheritance duties are within the jurisdiction of the Regions. They can therefore vary. In Flanders an amendment was recently approved by which people who had a permanent rela-tionship could inherit as cheaply as if they were married. The partners must have drawn up a will and have lived together for at least a year. Couples who have signed a cohabitation contract need not even have lived together for a year. In the other Regions changes to the laws on inheritance are in the pipeline.

Frédéric Antoine

The Belgian Economy

Discreet and Modest but International and Efficient

Who, at the start of the 21st century, is the mightiest Belgian? Beyond the inner circles of the initiated and business people, virtually no-one knows him. And he is delighted with the fact. As living proof that a person's importance is not connected with his fame, Albert Frère starts each day with the motto "to live happily, you must live privately". Not a home-grown adage but in a small country it would appear to be extremely appropriate.

We know hardly anything about him except that he is crazy about golf and has a good nose for wine. In 1998 he even took over half of Château Cheval-Blanc, one of the rare St. Emilion premiers crus classés A. And the Château Rieussec has already caught his eye. Who would ever have predicted that the son of a dealer in nails from the Charleroi area would make the kind of career for himself, which is practically unequalled in Europe? From his office in Loverval, a suburb of the old industrial city, Albert Baron Frère still keeps a strong hold on the reins of his favourite holding, the heavyweight Compagnie Nationale à Portefeuille (CPN). This was the springboard from which he, gifted with an innate commercial instinct, initially launched himself, into the steel industry. He left this "heavy" sector in time and invested his immense fortune in top Belgian companies. Thereafter he decided to trade and invest on a European scale.

Via the Pargesa/Groep Brussel-Lambert/Electrafina group, which he controls together with the Canadian Power (Desmarais family), Frère has substantial or even majority shares in companies operating worldwide: Total Fina (6th largest oil company in the world), the Suez Lyonnaise des Eaux company, Bertelsman the multimedia giant (umbrella organisation of the audiovisual enterprise RTL-Group, among others) and the Imetal company.

126

Albert Frère
© Van Parys Media

Via the CNP, Frère also manages medium-sized companies in the food, energy, publishing and media sectors, exceptional distribution and luxury products. For example, he has pumped new blood into Dupuis publishing, one of the flagships of the Belgian comic strip. Dupuis is the birthplace of Spirou and Fantasio, Lucky Luke, the Smurfs and Gaston Lagaffe. Frère made them the major publisher of the French-language comic strip, at least in terms of the number of publications. In the food sector, Frère owns Entremont French cheeses, part of the production of another Belgian symbol: waffles (Suzy and Corona Lotus), the Belgian ice cream producer IJsboerke, and Van Parijs, the Belgian chocolate maker. And we have not yet mentioned the range of English luxury ready-to-wear clothes, to which he attaches great importance.

As the king of Belgian high finance with an increasingly European profile, Albert Frère is the spiritual heir to the long line of intrepid entrepreneurs who, since the beginning of the industrial revolution, have endowed Belgium with worldwide fame. Just to put this into perspective: a subtle strategy for owner/management has gained the upper hand over pure production targets. And a somewhat calculated respect for moderation has replaced the opulent lifestyle with which the industrial big shots of the past liked to make themselves conspicuous.

Ingenious Engineers

Perhaps we have forgotten, but in 1910 Belgium was the world's third greatest trading nation. Our country exported its rails, carriages, locomotives, trams...to all corners of the world. At the end of the 19th century the southern part of Russia was even regularly referred to as a "Belgian industrial province".

The country has its businessmen and engineers to thank for this rapid climb to fame. Cockerill piloted Belgium into the Industrial Age with its steam machines. Coppée ruled over the coal-mines and coke ovens. Nagelmackers invented the sleeper train. Solvay conquered the world with his sodium carbonate, a product which was clearly a good alternative to the scarce natural soda. In 1904 Edward Empain, a teacher's son, established ACEC (Ateliers de Construction Electrique de Charleroi). During the same period he constructed electrical power stations in Russia, Brazil, Egypt and China. He introduced local railways to these countries, as he did in France, where he built the Paris metro. Having acquired a taste for grandeur, he went on to make Heliopolis, the mythical town just outside Cairo, rise up out of the desert sands. 5,000 hectares of desert were turned into streets and linked by tram to the capital city. At the same time, Jadot and Francqui were introducing the railway civilisation into China by constructing the 1,200 kilometres of track between Beijing and Hankow in just four years. Frankignoul invented the post named after him. The world belonged to the Belgians, that fearless race of conquerors.

Lieven Gevaert
AMSAB

A century later many of these enterprises have become international and often their capital is only partially in Belgian hands. Nevertheless, the names of many famous industrialists or brands continue to spread the Belgian image. That of the Englebert dynasty, for instance, which founded the first Belgian car-tyre factory in 1898. Or Alphonse Emmens, who acquired the Eternit licence from the Austrian industrialist Ludwig Hatschek and thought of the idea of reinforcing cement with fibres. Donnay International stepped out of the golden age of the tennis racket and into the production of sports requisites. Glaverbel is a reference point in the world of glass. And besides that there is the chocolate of Côte d'Or, Jacquemotte coffee, Pacha chicory, sugar from Tienen, matches from Union Match, the Saint-Roch cast-iron heating boilers.

Mortsel, close to Antwerp, still honours the memory of that amazing entrepreneur Lieven (Livinus) Gevaert (1868-1935), even though the products which brought him fame have been produced since 1964 by the Agfa-Gevaert company, an affiliate of the Bayer group. When he was 14, Gevaert opened a small photographic shop with his mother. On 28th June 1894 he founded "Lieven Gevaert & Co.", a company specialising in photographic paper, made by a new process. His reputation and fortune were made. Gevaert paper was used throughout the world, later films and cameras were added and later still the photocopiers which, at least partially, in their 'Gevafax' label, still carry the name of the inventor from the metropolis.

Other entrepreneurs whose companies still retains their Belgian roots, have accepted the support of international capital. Since 1961, for instance, Janssen Pharmaceutica has been part of the American giant Johnson & Johnson, but no less a jewel in the crown of Belgian know-how in the pharmaceutical sector. The company takes its name from its founder, Doctor Paul Janssen. He started his laboratories in Turnhout in 1954. Since then "Doctor Paul's" research teams have developed almost 80 new medicines. Five of them are on the WHO list of "250 indispensable medicines". This pharmaceutical enterprise is represented in some 40 countries and in 1985, as the first in its sector, in China.

Paul Janssen
Foto: Janssen Pharmaceutica

Brilliant in the Detail

Belgian charisma is not based on boasting. The list of names connected with Belgian inventiveness or with the typical Belgian commercial instinct could be boldly extended. For instance, the world leaders in the chalk market are two Belgian companies, Carmeuse and Lhoist. The first was founded in 1860 in Liège and is considered the largest producer of all kinds of chalk, with almost a hundred factories in more than 20 countries. The second, founded by Hippolyte Dumont in 1889, established an outlet in France in 1926 and penetrated the American market in 1981. The professionals in dredging and off-shore construction are Belgians, too. Deme and Jan De Nul are companies who are successors to concerns started shortly before the Second World War. At the start of the 21st century they are present in all the large international markets. Since 1934 the Kortrijk company Barco has distinguished itself in the communications sector. Having started out as producers of televisions, it is now the unchallenged specialist in large-screen video projectors. The company IBA (Ion Beam Applications), a spin-off of the nuclear research laboratories of the Catholic University of Leuven is once again an international authority in the field of mini-cyclotrons. This young "miracle" company has climbed to the top at lightning speed from its beginning as a small enterprise.

Alongside these giants it is often in the details, the little things, that Belgians show themselves to excel. They make small items, sometimes scarcely visible, but nonetheless essential. This is the case with the wire-drawing company of Leo Leander Bekaert, a small concern when it was founded in 1880, now developed into an international enterprise, the first producer and independent distributor, on a world scale, of steel wire and high-quality fence wire. Throughout the world people quench their thirst from glasses made in Zinnik, where production started in 1898: the realisation of an industrial dream by Baron Janssens. Originally the glasses were made by the Compagnie Internationale de Gobeleterie Inébréchable. Since 1935, when the switch was made from hand-blowing to machine-blowing, they have been called "Durobor". The glass was cut warm at that time, but a small ridge was formed along the edge. The glass was harder there (*dur au bord*) but also stronger. The company directors of the time made a sales advantage out of the production fault. They called their glass "Durobor", a name which is still used, although the company, now connected with the Ravenhead organisation, produces a wide range of glasses in Belgium: wine glasses, beer glasses, glasses for long drinks, whisky, ice cream, cocktails, champagne, etc. At St. Amands, on the bank of the river Scheldt, the Guma range of children's shoes came into being as the brainchild of Antwerp's Roger Maes. He studied shoe design at the Ars Sutoria school in Milan. Today he also makes shoes in Italy, Spain and Portugal. Driving into a car park, passing the barrier, is often only possible thanks to the monitoring and admission equipment designed in the Wavre factory owned by Michel Coenraets from Rixensart. The first Automatic Systems barriers were installed in Brussels in 1969. Since then you are likely to come across them in underground railway stations in Manila, Madrid, Ankara, Barcelona, Kuala Lumpur, Toronto, Singapore, Buenos Aires and Guanajuanto and on toll motorways in the People's Republic of China, Mexico and Chile.

Small fireworks were and still remain a speciality of Liège. Their fame has been built by handmade articles produced by the FN, the Fabrique Nationale d'Armes de Guerre. The concern was formed in 1889. Some ten arms manufacturers from Liège joined forces to meet an order from the Belgian army for 150,000 Mauser guns. FN's celebrity in the field of weapon design for warfare has continued to grow since then. But the enterprise acquired an enviable reputation between the wars with the production of hunting weapons, motor bikes, lorries and cars. After a number of reorganisations FN still remains a reference point today in the light weapons sector.

Eighty per cent of all billiard balls in
the world are made in and around
Tournai

Smaller, and less dangerous: 80 per cent of all billiard balls produced on the planet are of Belgian manufacture. The balls are made near Doornik from Saluc phenolic resin and marketed under different names. Even smaller: priding itself on 150 years of local know-how, a number of independent producers united in 1970 in Turnhout to form the CartaMundi company, which has become the European leader in the playing card market. The company produces 185 million packs annually, or 200 cards per second. The smallest of all cards is the "electronic purse'", the "Proton card". This is also a Belgian idea developed jointly by Banksys and the banks. It is working its way into wallets throughout the world.

Belgium is playing a leading role in the development of electronic payment
Photo: Banksys

Voyages Of Discovery And Inventions

Humble and Practical Inventors

It is indisputable: Belgians have been proving for centuries that they can invent very solid and usable items. That certainly applies to the chemist Leo Hendrik Baekeland, born in Ghent on 14 November 1863, who later became a naturalised American. Having developed a photographic paper which could be quickly developed, for which he sold the rights to Eastman, he worked with synthetic resins. In 1907 he developed one of the first modern plastics. It carried his own name: bakelite. At first this new material was used for electrical insulation, but it gradually penetrated all aspects of modern life. Some 36 years earlier, Zénobe Gramme had given cyclists the gift of light with the first dynamo-electrical generator capable of converting mechanical energy into electrical energy: the birth of the dynamo. This inventor, born in Jehay and working in Paris, signed the death warrant of steam power: he made it possible for electricity to replace it. Joseph Plateau from Ghent (1801-1883) was searching for the secret of the moving image. In 1833 he developed the forerunner of the film: the phenakistiscope, a revolving disc which created the illusion of movement. Some also attribute the invention of the first stroboscope, in 1836, to him. But it is not certain whether Plateau could claim this invention. He is, though, the one who thought out retinal persistence. He tested this hypothesis with such zeal that, by looking at the sun too often, he finally went blind.

Leo Baekeland
The Man Who Invented Plastics

AMSAB / © Publi Presse

The invention of plastics was a milestone in the history of chemistry. Leo Baekeland, as the inventor of bakelite, has therefore won a place among the most influential scientists of the 20th century. He was born in Ghent in 1863, the son of a shoemaker. Baekeland did well at school and went on to read natural sciences at Ghent University, where he graduated with honour. After his graduation he taught there as an assistant, while working on inventions in his spare time.

In 1889 he went to the United States on his honeymoon. Leo Baekeland was very impressed by the opportunities and dynamism of that country, and the newly married couple decided to emigrate. He immediately found a job in the chemical industry, and soon set up his own small chemicals business. He had a feel for the needs of the market and in 1895 improved the already familiar photographic printing paper by making it sensitive to artificial light. His Velox photographic paper was received enthusiasti-

cally in the recently developed photographic industry, and in 1899 he was able to sell his business to Eastman Kodak for the phenomenal sum of US 1 million.

At a stroke Baekeland had become a rich man and he moved with his wife and two children to New York, where he carried on with his experiments in his own laboratory. In 1906, in his search for a covering for electric wiring, he invented bakelite, the first completely chemically manufactured synthetic material. The age of chemistry and plastics had begun. Bakelite was very soon used on a massive scale for the production of all kinds of appliances. Within a few years' time, objects made of bakelite, ranging from telephones to boxes and other household articles, were to be found in almost every home. Leo Baekeland became a professor at Columbia University and later President of the National Association of Chemists. He died in 1944 in the United States, his adopted country.

133

While we are dealing with "useful inventions," we should certainly mention Antoine-Joseph Sax (Adolphe to his friends) from Dinant. This instrument builder, both a productive and brilliant inventor, improved a large number of existing instruments and experimented with a number of others. He was so inventive that, at the 1840 Brussels Exhibition, where he showed nine of his inventions, he was denied the award of first prize on the pretext that he was too young and that there would be nothing to offer him the following year. This was all Sax needed to emigrate to Paris. It was there, in 1842 at 30 years of age, that he became known as the father of the saxophone. Berlioz was an enthusiastic proponent of the new invention. But Sax had to defend it in court against all manner of imitations. Bizet, Wagner, Puccini, Ravel and Satie all held the instrument in high esteem but it was jazz musicians in particular who provided it with a permanent place in history. The honour after a long battle, fought alone by one man.

Dreams of Space

Belgians, gasping for breath on account of their claustrophobically small country, have always dreamed of going out into the big, wide world and getting to know the wide-open spaces. The geographer Mercator (1512-1594), inventor of cartography and the planisphere, showed them the way. Since then they have continued to follow in his footsteps. Hot on the heels of Tintin, the journalist who was just as much an anthropologist as the one who discovered the planet's mysteries. Or by immersing themselves in the adventures of Bob Morane by Henri Vernes. Or smiling at Max the explorer's jokes, the comic strip hero from Bara and son of a Belgian diplomat. Or by more or less recognising themselves in the style of the "Belgian explorer" who, according to Greystoke, discovered a certain Tarzan, brought up in the jungle by a female ape, and who brought civilisation to the world.

Gerard Mercator
Stedelijke Musea Sint-Niklaas

The economic motivation is obvious, but there must have been something else like a thirst for immeasurable spaces to explain why the Belgians threw themselves so enthusiastically into the golden age of their colonialism. How else can we explain the passion with which the seafarer Adrien de Gerlache de Gomery explored the area around the South Pole where, in 1898, with the crew of the "Belgica", he was the first to spend the winter? Or grasp the stubbornness which ignited the spirit of Wim Verstraeten, the balloonist who attempted to fly around the world together with his companion, the Swiss Bertrand Piccard?

Conquering space is just as much a Belgian preoccupation as conquering the Earth. One of the specialists who helped Piccard bring the journey with the Breitling Orbiter 3 to a successful conclusion, was the Belgian meteorologist Luc Trullemans. Auguste Piccard, Bertrand Piccard's grandfather, who penetrated the stratosphere in 1931 in a balloon and then plunged to the bottom of the sea in a bathyscaph, was a professor at the Free University of Brussels. In

Adolphe Sax
Inventor of the Saxophone

Antoine-Joseph Sax, that was the real name of the inventor of the saxophone, was born in Dinant in 1814. He was a chip off the old block. His father had a large workshop where wind instruments were made and Adolphe, as he called himself, became an apprentice there. He had talent: by the time he was 16 he had already produced the first instrument he designed himself. In the next few years he improved the bass clarinet and designed the "saxhorn" among other things, but his best known invention came later. In 1840 he played his saxophone for the first time, hidden behind a curtain, because he did not have a patent for it yet and was afraid of imitators. The French King Louis Philippe heard of the miraculous instrument and invited him to Paris to make instruments for his military bands. Two years later Adolphe had a workshop in the French capital and in 1846 obtained a patent for his saxophone. He did not work only on musical instruments; he also made an improved steam whistle for railway engines and designed an air conditioning unit. In addition to his work as an inventor and instrument maker, he also taught the saxophone, published music, and for a time led the brass section at the Paris Opera.

Adolphe Sax may have been a talented instrument maker, but he was not equally gifted in business. His whole life long he was entangled in court cases about licences and patents; they lost him a great deal of money and he went bankrupt several times. Yet with the help of influential friends he was always able to find the money to build his business up again. On his death in 1894 one of his sons took over his workshop but sold it some 20 years later to the well-known firm of Selmer, which still makes saxophones today. The saxophone remained Sax's most important achievement. The instrument became famous after the First World War, when it was discovered by the world of jazz. It is still popular and is appreciated across the world, because it is so expressive and capable of reflecting the emotions of the musician.

The jazz scene in Belgium is flourishing

Dirk Frimout
© Van Parys Media

the Belgium of the 1930s he was so popular that Hergé was inspired by him when creating the character Professor Calculus. This type of academic crosses our path on other occasions, personified by the great Belgian research scientists. Take, for instance, the first Belgian astronaut, Dirk Frimout! This Doctor in Applied Physics was responsible for the scientific experiments during the Atlas 1 flight by the space-shuttle Atlantis. He stirred up Belgian passions by telling them stories of his adventure with childlike amazement.

You also need to be a Belgian in order to enjoy peering into the heavens, just like Adolphe Quetelet, who founded the Belgian Observatory in 1823. Quetelet is known throughout the world for his fundamental research. He is the father of modern statistical science, a branch of mathematics which is concerned with the calculation of probabilities. You would also need to have been a Belgian and a dreamer who yearns for distant horizons to have invented the roller skate, the forerunner of roller blades. A certain John Joseph Merlin from Hoei hit upon the idea. According to certain sources he designed his machine by mounting wheels under his clogs, enabling him to move through London streets at greater speed. Others claim that he whirled through the salons playing the violin, an art he mastered with virtuosity. Being of Belgian extraction was clearly also a prerequisite for inventing the trolley-bus. Major metropolises with traffic arteries on steep slopes support their claim to an "ecological" image by still putting to use this original, environmentally friendly means of transport. Charles J. Van Depoele (1846-1892), a Belgian who became a naturalised American, thought of the idea in the United States, in Richmond and then in Chicago. This fanatic of electricity, founder of the Van Depoele Electric Co. finally introduced his invention to Toronto. It is from there that the trolley reached Europe. Liège was so enthusiastic that its public transport company chose the trolley in preference to the ordinary bus.

137

Both Van Depoele and Merlin remain underestimated. The same can be said of the Belgian father of the famous Big Bang theory of the constant expansion of the universe. Nowadays it is customary to ascribe this relativistic cosmology to Edwin Hubble and Albert Einstein. Nevertheless, the first formulations were the work of the Russian Alexander Friedmann and the Belgian Father Georges Lemaître (1894-1966). His ideas attained some success in the 1930s and his name did the rounds in the scientific world. But afterwards, this canon who was not so happy at not being seen as a saint in his own country, ended up in virtually complete obscurity. And his work was never awarded a Nobel Prize.

A Caring Country

Looking After The Bodies

It must be that the inheritance of Andreas Vesalius, Charles V's doctor and father of modern anatomy, it still setting the tone, because five of the nine Nobel Prizes awarded to Belgians are closely connected with the field of medicine and physiology. Jules Bordet received the Prize in 1919 for his discoveries in immunology; Corneille Heymans in 1938 for his study of the role of the sinus and the blood vessels in regulating breathing; Albert Claude and Christian Duve in 1974 for their contribution to the knowledge of the structure and operation of the internal parts of cells.

As a thermodynamicist, Ilya Prigogine, who received the Nobel Prize for Chemistry in 1977 for his innovative theory of dissipative structures, falls rather outside the trend in the company of these "medical" types. In this field even more Belgians shine. Dr Peter Piot, for instance, internationally acknowledged as an authority in the fight against AIDS, became an special member of the American Institute of Medicine in 2000. Since 1994 he has been heading up the United Nations organisation, co-ordinating the battle against the dreadful disease at an international level.

Striving to do everything to attain better health is a permanent commitment in Belgium. For example, in 1999, Walter Fiers' team (Ghent University) succeeded in perfecting a universal vaccine against the flu. And earlier there had been the discovery by Jeff Schell and Marc van Montagu, two biologists who in the early 1980s achieved the first plant transgenesis by replacing the genes in a microbe responsible for a tumour with other genes.

Peter Piot
UNAIDS

Care Of The Heart

You need not be a scientist or a physician to devote attention to others. That was proven by Father Damiaan De Veuster, the lepers' apostle, on Molokai. Everywhere that leprosy still rages, the Damiaan Foundation continues his work. The same is true for the Vredeseilanden – Islands of Peace. In Hoei and Namur, The Aid to Displaced Persons and the University of Peace carries

AMSAB / © Belga

Ilya Prigogine
Nobel Prize Winner (Chemistry)

Ilya Prigogine's life work was ambitious: to reformulate the laws of physics. Classical Newtonian physics sees the world as determined by unalterable laws, but Prigogine wanted a science which left room for uncertainty, chance and creativity, starting from a new appreciation of time.

Ilya Prigogine was born in Moscow in the historic year 1917. Four years later his parents fled Russia and after years of wandering settled in Brussels. Little Ilya seemed destined for the "soft sciences'": he could decipher musical notation and play the piano before he could read, and was fascinated by philosophy, history and archaeology. He studied Latin and Greek, but when he was confronted with the sciences, he was mesmerised by the absence of the concept of time in all the theories. The problem intrigued him so much that he went to Brussels University to read chemistry and physics. He was to study, earn his doctorate and teach

there. In 1946 he first put forward his theory of thermodynamics with irreversible processes. It was met with disbelief and contempt. Prigogine went on working and in 1977 was rewarded by the Nobel Prize for Chemistry.

Prigogine published several scientific bestsellers, taught at the universities of Chicago and Texas and since 1959 has been head of the Solvay Institute in Brussels. International recognition has brought him an almost endless list of prizes and honorary degrees. Although Prigogine's work is contested by some people, it is still recognised as pioneering. It lay at the basis of Chaos Theory, which assumes that in a situation of instability elements have a tendency to organise themselves. The theory in its turn has had a great influence on a whole range of disciplines, not only in the exact sciences, but also in the life sciences.

on the work of Father Dominique Pire. This advocate of better understanding between peoples won a Nobel Prize in 1958, after he had devoted himself to refugees from the East. More recently, in 1971, Madeleine Cinquin, known as Sister Emmanuelle, settled in the Cairo slums. This nun, a member of the Order of Our Lady of Sion, who was born in Brussels in 1908, shared her life with these ragged creatures until her retirement in 1993 and thus showed her iron will to act in the heart of despair.

AMSAB / © Belga

Father Damien
Hero of the Lepers

Joseph de Veuster, born in 1840 in Tremelo, was one of the many Flemings who in the 19th century wanted to devote their life to religion. When he was 18 he became a member of the Congregation of the Sacred Hearts of Jesus and Mary, and chose "Damien" as his monastic name. He had almost completed his training as a priest when he learnt that priests were needed in the Sandwich Islands, now Hawaii. He was allowed to leave, and in 1863 he arrived in Honolulu, where he continued his training and was ordained priest.

His career as a priest began in Hawaii itself, but after nine years he went to work temporarily in the leper colony on the neighbouring island of Molokai. When he arrived there in 1873 he found utter chaos, with the sick completely abandoned to their fate. Father Damien was not to be deterred. He visited and nursed the sick, organised their villages, arranged fitting funerals. What had started as a temporary job became a calling. Father Damien committed himself to spend the rest of his life among the lepers. He slowly but surely gained recognition and support from the authorities and from financial backers, so that he could start larger projects: an orphanage, doctors, a proper harbour, new roads, and even a musical society and a racecourse. When in 1884 a doctor diagnosed leprosy in him too, Father Damien became a patient among his patients. He died in 1889, having lived nearly 16 years with the horrors of leprosy.

Over the years, Father Damien had become well-known throughout the world and his death struck a very sympathetic chord. He was praised for his sacrifice and his humanity, and many organisations continued to give financial support for the work he had started. In 1935 it was decided to bring his body back to Louvain, and when the ship tied up in Antwerp, even King Leopold III himself was there to welcome his mortal remains. Damien's deeds are still not forgotten. In 1995 he was beatified and the procedures for his canonisation have now been started.

The interest in the Third World and welcoming others still inspire the Belgian sections of Médecins sans Frontières and Oxfam. These foreign organisations chose Belgium among others to open the first branches outside their own borders. And there are still many Belgian clergy who devote their lives to helping others and who leave for foreign countries under assignment from their missions.

Closer to home, too, there is a striving for solidarity. Shortly after the Second World War, Father Froidure founded the Petits Sapins en Stations de Plein Air. These are homes for young people rejected by their own society. Froidure's work was undoubtedly inspired by Cardinal Jozef Cardijn (1882-1967). As the child of a worker's family from Schaarbeek, Cardijn was sensitive from an early age to the suffering caused by industrialisation. In 1912, as Vicar of Laken, close to Brussels, he formed his first group of young labourers. Together with them, he set up "working groups who think about the facts, with a view to action". This led to the famous motto "see, judge, act". "Basing oneself on facts, investigating the situation, becoming aware of the dignity of God's worker-son, change the unfair lifestyle and working circumstances." In 1925, Cardijn's work led to the founding of the KAJ, an international militant and Catholic movement which strives for social justice and is based on respect and dignity for each and every person, in the spirit of evangelism. Even though the KAJ is now less popular among the younger generations of workers, this organisation's influence within the Catholic Church remains enormous. This is especially true through its Third World presence.

Complaints About Social Inequalities

The priest Adolf Daens was, within the social movement, a forerunner of Jozef Cardijn. His political efforts on behalf of Aalst's poorest received mixed reactions in 19th-century Belgium. Stijn Coninx filmed his story in 1992. Furthermore, Belgian film-makers have always made a point of complaining about social inequalities and brought "real" life into focus. In the 1930s Henri Storck was the first master of the Belgian documentary film and has always shone in his ability to set up his camera in the middle of real life. The cult film *Borinage*, which Storck made with Joris Ivens about the misery of ordinary man, is still relevant as a valid example in this category

The most recent films, too, show that social stirrings still exist. After they had made themselves heard with La Promesse, the brothers Luc and Jean-Pierre Dardenne received the Golden Palm Award at the 25th Cannes Festival for Rosetta. This film tells the story of an 18-year old girl who finds shelter on a campsite and fights for a normal life and recognition as a human being. Emilie Dequenne received the prize for best actress. Three years earlier the young

Downs-Syndrome actor Pascal Duquenne received the same award for his role in *Le Huitième Jour*, both human and moving, which gave proof of concern for social questions. The same is true for the Palm awarded to Natacha Règnier in 1998 for her achievement in *La Vie Rêvée des Anges*. Frank van Passel's *Manneken Pis*, in which Antje de Boeck played the tram driver, fits into this style, which path had formerly been trodden by film-makers like Robbe de Hert and Marian Handwerker. "Normal" life can inspire everything in films. Everything, including the everyday occurrences, which together form the fictional intrigue of the film *C'est arrivé près de Chez Vous* (1992) by Rémy Belvaux and Benoît Poelvoorde. The unreal and unbelievable emerge from reality as it really is. It is sufficient to observe this, as Chantal Ackerman from Brussels continues to do since her film Jeanne Dielman, 23 Quai du Commerce, 1080, Brussels (1975). Or to uncover reality in an attempt to show people as they really are. This is what Jean Libon and Marco Lamensch have been trying to do for ten years with their gruesome television portraits in *Striptease*. This television concept, unique in its style, was inspired by the trend of *réalité-fiction*, which has been developed on French-language television since the 1970s by Pierre Manuel and Jean-Jacques Péché, and thereafter by the brilliant cameraman-reporter, Manu Bonmariage.

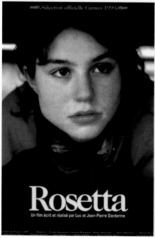

The Dardenne brothers' 'Rosetta' was so moving that Minister Onkelinx's social plan was called after it.
© Jean-François Tefnin

Stijn Coninx's film 'Daens' won an Oscar
Favourite Films

Toto the hero

© Belga

Jean-Claude van Damme
Actor

143

Because Jean-Claude van Varenberg, born in Brussels in 1960, was a puny boy with glasses, he was bullied at school. So that he could defend himself, his parents sent him to karate lessons. This was a success. The fragile Jean-Claude trained six hours a day and developed an impressive and limber body. After training as a window dresser – he learnt to make very fetching flower arrangements – he opened a fitness centre. The enterprise was soon making a profit, but Jean-Claude wanted more. He wanted to become an actor and decided to try his luck in Hollywood. Van Varenberg became "Van Damme'" because that name still revealed his Belgian roots, but was easier to pronounce for Americans.

For nearly two years Van Damme survived as a porter, chauffeur, masseur and so forth, while he learnt English and haunted casting offices. One day he met the head of a large production company making cheap action films. The self-assured Jean-Claude immediately gave him a sample of what he could do. It wor- ked. He was given the lead in the very gory picture *Bloodsport*. The film was more successful than expected and the karate expert won several more leading roles in cheap, violent karate films. After a few years the big studios realised that there was money to be made with him, and he was given a few roles in larger films. Jean-Claude had become a celebrity, "Muscles from Brussels" a catchword.

The new star enjoyed his success. He was at every party, surrounded himself with pretty women, and became hooked on cocaine. After one wild night almost ended with an over- dose, Jean-Claude decided to make drastic chan- ges in his life. He kicked the habit, divorced his fourth wife and starting rebuilding his body. He found peace in the arms of his third wife, Gladys Portugues, whom he remarried in Knokke in 1999. Since then Jean-Claude has been working on a comeback, and hopes again to become the darling of the public.

A Country in Motion

Successful Immigration

At the heart of Europe, Belgium is a meeting point for a variety of cultures. The successive waves of immigration have nourished our land with new tastes and new identities. Here, a child born in Morlanwelz of the Italian immigrant, Elio di Rupo, could become Deputy Premier without a problem, subsequently Minister-President of Wallonia and finally chairman of a political party. And there are other famous Belgians who originated from the Italian exodus. The producer Franco Dragone is one of them. He arrived in Belgium when he was eight, went to school in Quebec and now wants to make La Louvière a general headquarters for large-scale North American productions. The world famous Salvatore Adamo was three when, in 1947, he left Sicily, the area where he was born. He settled in Jemappes. 20 years later he had sold 20 million records, making him the most popular French-language singer of his generation. A number of his successes, like *Les filles du bord de mer*, inspired other artists who often belong to different musical styles. Keeping things in proportion, Adamo's fellow-countryman, Rocco Granata, achieved comparable success in the north of the country with a single song, Marina. In Adamo's wake, a good number of Italian Belgians attained fame with French chanson: Claude Barzotti, with his husky "Rital" voice, Frank Michaël, Frédéric François, alias Francesco Barracato, Sandra Caldarone, better known under the name Sandra Kim who won the Eurovision Song Contest in 1986, and Lara Fabian, born in

144

Cirque du Soleil, Franco Dragone © Belga   **Django Reinhardt** © Van Parys Media   **Philippe Catherine** © Iori De Windt

Etterbeek of a Sicilian mother and Belgian father. She emigrated and became a naturalised Canadian in 1996, in order to give her musical successes international allure.

This inclination to refresh oneself at foreign springs is also at the heart of the privileged place acquired by jazz in Belgium's cultural landscape. It might sound strange but this music, which came into being in the black ghettos of the southern United States of America, struck an immediate chord in our country, especially in the south. This was undoubtedly due to its expressive potential but also certainly because it could so well arouse a sense of melancholy.

Belgian jazz distinguishes itself not so much through its grace notes but rather through its tenderness and refinement. Its two most striking protagonists have made this perfectly clear. The virtuoso "gypsy" guitarist Jean-Baptiste (Django) Reinhardt (1910-1953), born in Liverchies, discovered a completely new way of playing his instrument. And Jean (Toots) Thielemans, the harmonica player born in Brussels in 1922, acquired the nickname Mr. Whistle thanks to his whistling talent. As the spearhead of "modern jazz" are the modest but widely respected Brussels guitarist Philip Catherine, Django's successor, and another famous guitar personality, René Thomas (1927-1975). This master of bebop was born in Liège, approximately a year after the tenor saxophonist Bobby Jaspar. He was also from Liège, as was the alto saxophonist Jacques Peltzer. Together with Steve Houben and Kurt Van Herck, all these musicians prove that Belgium manages Adolphe Sax's legacy extremely capably. But there are more Belgian jazz musicians who play other instruments with virtuosity: Sadi Lallemand the vibraphone, and Nathalie Loriers, Charles Loos and Michael Herr the piano...

Toots Thielemans
Musician

Jean 'Toots' Thielemans was born with exceptional musical talent. When barely three, he was already playing the accordion on the doorstep of his parents' café in the Marolles district of Brussels. Later he taught himself the harmonica, but finally opted for the guitar. Thielemans, born in 1922, first became involved with jazz around the time of the Second World War. He began experimenting with jazz and performed in small cafés where he acquired a name as a jazz guitar player. One day he also tried out some jazz on his harmonica. The bebop sounds Toots could coax out of that simple instrument were phenomenal. He could put so much feeling into it that everyone who heard it was carried along by the music. Toots was the first to play bebop on a mouth organ and made this his trademark. All who followed were imitating him.

In the early 1950s Toots went to America, because the source of jazz, particularly black music, was there. He found a job playing the guitar in a jazz quintet. To add something extra to his music, he occasionally whistled a jazz tune; this gimmick made him very popular. After five years he left the quintet and started several groups himself, usually playing the harmonica. This is when he got the name 'Toots', after two great jazz musicians before him, Toots Mondello and Toots Camanata.

Toots accepted all kinds of assignments: he composed music for commercials, contributed to numerous pop records, and wrote film music, of which the score for *Midnight Cowboy* is probably the best known. He played in select jazz groups, but for years he has also kept young children spellbound with his music for *Sesame Street*. Toots is completely at home in all genres. In spite of his age, he still plays regularly to packed houses and brings out new records. On stage he no longer plays the guitar, following a heart attack a few years ago, but the master's harmonica play-ing is still unequalled.

Everyone Sings

Not all popular music falls into the jazz category and not all famous Belgian singers are children of immigrants. For instance, our only fellow-citizen ever to score a number one hit in the American hit parade was a "real" Belgian: Jeannine Deckers, better known as Soeur Sourire or "The Singing Nun'" Her best-known song, *Dominique*, became a real rage in the 1960s. That other international artist, Jacques Brel, never enjoyed the privilege of being number one in the United States. But on the other hand, some of his successes were sung by other artists, who claimed the honour for themselves. Brel elected to make his "breakthrough" via Paris. Annie Cooreman, or Annie Cordie, born in Brussels in 1928, had preceded him in this. This cabaret artist had already realised that the City of Light was an inevitable stop in the domain of performing arts. And she certainly did not need to give up her "Belgianness" for this. Many artists took the same route. She developed her career in France and enjoyed official recognition there. Maurane was born in Brussels in 1960 into a family of musicians. Axelle Red (Hasselt, 1968) is a Law graduate who started singing in English before becoming a celebrity of French chanson. Or take Philippe Lafontaine (Gosselies, 1955) who started his career singing advertising jingles.

Axelle Red
© Goedefroit Music

Maurane
© Goedefroit Music

Famous and Memorable Belgians. These too are Belgians

© Van Parys Media

Jacques Brel
Chansonnier

Jacques Brel lived like one possessed. When he sang he threw his heart and soul out into his audience, and after every performance he dived into a bar where he drank and smoked as if it were his last day in this world. Yet he came from a respectable Brussels family and was, like his brother, destined to work in his father's cardboard factory. But that did not suit Jacques's rebellious nature. Although he was married and had two children, he wanted to escape from his middle class existence. He went off to Paris on his own and began to build a career as a singer, with very little success at first. Brel spent several years in miserable conditions and had to struggle to gain recognition for his songs.

The breakthrough came in 1957, when he won a song competition with *Quand on n'a que l'amour*. Brel fought against his past and in his lyrics sang about what interested him: love, his rejection of narrow-mindedness, and religion. His sincere lyrics and simple but compelling music appealed. At the peak of his success he was appearing 300 times a year and travelled all round the world.

1967 marked a turning point in his career. Brel no longer believed in the celebrity life and felt that he could only repeat himself. As a result he decided to make no more appearances. And he kept his word. He still worked in music. One of his activities was producing the musical *The Man from La Mancha* and he brought out several new records. Later Brel became interested in film, first as an actor, but later he directed several films himself. As the years slid by, Brel cut himself off more and more from the hectic world, until finally, with his girlfriend, Madly, he settled on an island in the Pacific. He spent his last years there until in 1978 he died of lung cancer.

Other Belgian singers preferred to remain in their *plat pays*. The group Clouseau, formed by Bob Savenberg in 1984 in Sint-Genesius Rode, has always kept its musical successes rooted in Belgian soil. Arno Hintjens from Ostend will never deny this choice: his Belgian identity is so clearly visible in his unparalleled legend of the cowboy-rocker that he is just as happy to give a rendition in English as in French.

In recent years Belgian pop has been enjoying great success. Groups like dEUS, Zita Swoon, K's Choice and Hooverphonic are right up at the top in terms of quality and are extremely popular, both at home and abroad. And is anyone "more Belgian" than our own Helmut Lotti, whose real name is Helmut Lotigiers? This perennially youthful number one with the golden voice, born in 1969, succeeds in seducing all generations in all languages with a repertory of popular classical melodies.

Belgium has a few big names in modern classical music, such as Pierre Bartholomée and Henri Pousseur. And it is here in Belgium, too, that the Queen Elizabeth Competition for

Famous and Memorable Belgians. These too are Belgians

Arno Hintjens
Musician

© Paul De Malsche

The uncrowned king of fusion music was trained as, of all things, a chef. He always hated school, and therefore Arno Hintjens went on a hotel training course because, for some reason or other, cooking appealed to him. Arno was born in 1945 – in a taxi – and grew up in Ostend. His father was horrified to see his dear son showing no respect for the riches he had fought for himself. Arno was a rebel and a non-conformist who wanted to enjoy life. From an early age he loved the world of music and played in several bands. Arno was always the leader and although he spoke with a stutter, this handicap disappeared as soon as he started to sing. The first group with which he created a stir was Tjens Couter, and from it developed the unsurpassed TC Matic.

Arno played because he could not help it, he was a born entertainer. All the money he could scrape together, he put into his music. TC Matic had a repertoire that had never been heard before. It was an amalgam of rock, funk and blues, but also of French chanson with something inherited from Belgian musical tradition. Through Herman Schueremans, the festival organiser, the group acquired a recording contract with EMI. Arno and his mates toured throughout Europe, and turned up on stage at virtually all the major festivals. From 1980 to 1986 they put Belgium on the map, and their music had an enormous influence on the European musical scene. They could have become world famous, but for that the group would have had to make concessions in their music and their attitude. This they consistently refused to do. TC Matic split up after six years of intensive work together.

Arno carried on solo. Other accents began to surface: influences from French music, but also Latin rhythms. Now and then he formed a temporary group for a tour. The latest of these was called Charles & the White Trash European Blues Connection. A name which perfectly reflects what he and his music stand for. In the intervals he writes film music and sometimes acts in a film. In spite of his success Arno still prefers to be bone idle and more than ever sees himself as a "deluxe dropout". Some things never change.

Barthold, Sigiswald and Wieland Kuijken
© Clem Willems

Bernard Foccroulle
© Belga

Herreweghe
llems

singing, piano and violin is so enthusiastically attended. There is admiration for the musical film in which director Gérard Corbiaux has specialised: Le Maître de Musique, Farinelli, and Le Roi Danse. But Belgians are especially crazy about singers with a voice. Lotti's success proves that, but the popularity of the Brussels tenor José van Dam and of Jules Bastin, who died in December 1996, does too.

In the revival of early music, Belgian musicians have played a pioneering role. Jos van Immerseel and the brothers Sigiswald, Barthold and Wieland Kuijken have explored new avenues by their execution of baroque music on historical instruments. Philippe Herreweghe applied new insights to vocal music and made his choir Collegium Vocale one of the best interpreters of Bach's music. Paul van Nevel specialised in the music of the late Middle Ages and early Renaissance. He brought back to life many compositions which were no longer played with his Huelgas Ensemble. Gradually the early-music specialists applied their insights to music from later periods. Belgium also hosts major festivals of early music, such as the Musica Antiqua in Bruges and Laus Polyphoniae in Antwerp. It is surely no coincidence that an opera melody – "The Saintly Love for the Fatherland" from *The Mute from Portici* – unleashed the Belgian Revolution in 1830.

Famous and Memorable Belgians. These too are Belgians

AMSAB / © Graphopresse

Queen Elizabeth
Queen Of The Belgians

Queen Elizabeth was born in 1876 to a Bavarian ducal family related to the Coburgs, of which the Belgian royal family were also members. She enjoyed a liberal education and was very interested in nature, science, culture and music. She would have liked to be a doctor like her father, but became a nurse, because no women were then accepted in medical schools. In 1900 she married Albert, Crown Prince of Belgium. It was an arranged marriage, but developed into a true love match.

In 1909 Albert succeeded Leopold II as King of the Belgians. Unlike their predecessors, the young royal couple appeared regularly in public, which made them both very popular. The King and Queen were also interested in social issues and took a number of charitable initiatives. During the First World War Elizabeth and Albert remained in beleaguered Belgium. Elizabeth was loved by the people because of her continued presence at the front as a nurse. This was the start of the legend of the Nurse Queen .

After the War, Elizabeth remained prominent in the world of culture and science.

She was particularly fascinated by Egyptian art and in 1923 was present at the opening of Tutankhamun's tomb. In Belgium she inspired the building of the Palais des Beaux Arts and initiated the Ysaye competition, later called the Queen Elizabeth Competition, for young musicians.

In 1934 Albert was killed in a climbing accident at Marche-les-Dames in the Ardennes and their eldest son succeeded him as Leopold III. The events of the Second World War were such that Leopold became no longer acceptable as king, and this painful period was only brought to an end by the accession of his son Baudouin in 1951.

From then on Elizabeth spent most of her time on the arts and travelling. She was fascinated by Eastern Europe and China and made regular visits there at the peak of the Cold War, consequently acquiring the nickname of the Red Queen. When she died of a heart attack in 1965, Belgium lost the first queen whose name and face were familiar to all her people.

Marc Reynebeau

Patriots in Spite of Everything

In the mid-1960s, the artist Marcel Broodthaers created several remarkable works of art, such as *La Valise Belge* (The Belgian Suitcase) or *Fémur d'homme Belge* (Femur of a Belgian Man). The titles make a direct reference to Belgium, and the colours in which the works are made denote the national black-yellow-red. Homage to the fatherland? Certainly not at first sight. The depiction is too humble for that, the tone of the works too scornful.

Broodthaers was by no means the first to turn out motifs like this. A couple of decades earlier, James Ensor, for example, liked working "national" elements into his paintings: flags, slogans, even the portrayal of rulers. For him, just as for Broodthaers, Belgium was a valid symbol of an extremely ambivalent lifestyle, a social arrangement, a mentality, from all of which he wanted to distance himself. And that resulted in a love-hate relationship which, on closer inspection, stemmed in the first place from an estrangement from authority. Which is, furthermore, always a good source for the production of art with integrity. Counter to the usual run of things, the many-side artist Hugo Claus gave ministers the change to speak in one of his poems:

> *"Poets are," say the ministers, "nit-pickers.*
> *Moaning about the soul. What good is that to the common man?*
> *Con-struc-tive thinking is not involved.*
> *Because what poet ever speaks about – you'll laugh, go ahead –*
> *Our E3-motorway which has cost a fortune*
> *And in prin-ci-ple can inspire just as much aesthetic emotion*
> *As the sea, the Scheldt, or a mother's breast?*
> *Or about our green areas, if you want to stay in the nature sector.*
> *Or about our art of carpet-weaving, famous as far as Detroit."*

The ambivalent attitude of Belgian artists to their fatherland is perhaps best expressed in the title of an anthology of literary articles which has become a classic, which appeared in 1980 on the occasion of Belgium's 150th birthday. *La Belgique malgré tout*, Belgium in spite of everything. Since the country, yes the nation, gets substantial attention from artists, it has developed steadily into an artistic motif. In short, it is a principle that occupies and inspires creative minds. Claus' major and internationally acclaimed novel *Het Verdriet van België* (*The Sorrow of Belgium*) does not carry that title for nothing. In fact, on its cover it reproduces part of an Ensor painting, in which the "tricolour" tints dominate. So yes, Belgium's OK, but you also have to include its everyday, small and on occasion less attractive perspective – which explains the "sorrow".

The "national" weather, as the vernacular likes to have it, is a shower of rain – *la drache nationale*, which for preference buckets down on 21 July, the national holiday. As far as this is concerned, there is a striking parallel between the majority of – also internationally important – Belgian artists and the bulk of the population. Most Belgians are really only lukewarm patriots, too level-headed and business-minded to let themselves get dragged along in nationalistic sentiment. Similarly, neighbouring countries have never had much trouble with Belgium. Even the Belgian colonial adventure in the Congo was never able to drum up much national enthusiasm. Only the royal family or amazing achievements by Belgian athletes can spur the almost unknown potential for occasional flag-waving into action, just as major catastrophes awaken a spontaneous form of national solidarity, but that is usually as far as it goes. And running alongside it, there is no unadulterated "national" art, no great literary or expressive works, no songs or monuments which sing the country's praises. It is certainly a subject for reflection but not an object of adoration.

HUGO CLAUS
HET VERDRIET
VAN BELGIË
ROMAN

DE BEZIGE BIJ

top: Hugo Claus
© Van Parys Media
bottom: The Sorrow of Belgium

© Nicole Hellyn

Marguerite Yourcenar (1903-1987)
Writer

Although Belgian by virtue of being born in Brussels (more specifically at 193 Avenue Louise) and having a Belgian mother (Fernande de Cartier de Marchienne, born in Suarlée, who, however, became French on her marriage), Marguerite de Crayencour, unlike her half-brother Michel Fernand, did not opt for Belgian nationality when she came of age. None the less her links with Belgium were not restricted to these particulars. She was often wrongly taken to be a Belgian, even by the members of the Académie Française. Marguerite Yourcenar herself referred to 'the languid Flemish ardour' of her origins, and she contrasted it with the 'sort of dry matter-of-factness, a dogged industry and acquisitiveness, quick-witted but at the same time small-minded, which characterizes the French provinces almost everywhere' (*Archives du Nord*). Apart from that she always kept up very close links with Belgian friends: Suzanne Lilar, Georges Sion, Carlo Bronne, André Delvaux, Guido Burggraeve, Alexis Curvers, Jacques Errera, Sonia de Saint-Hubert, Jean de Walque, and others.

The 'Passage Marguerite Yourcenar', recently held in the Rue au Laines in the centre of Brussels, included quotations from *L'Oeuvre au Noir*, Yourcenar's best known and most successful novel, for which she was awarded the Femina Prize in 1968. It is also her most 'Belgian' novel, because the action takes place mainly in Bruges. Those familiar with the work of the first lady member of the Académie Française will know that she was not always sympathetic towards Belgium, and certainly not to Belgian cities, which, like so many cities of the world, were polluted. Moreover, this country was too closely associated with her father's family. Yet the evocation of the ancient Flemish town in Yourcenar's novel is very successful. She makes it a imagined setting for the life of the imaginary family to which she would have liked to have belonged. And Zeno, the book's hero, was always like a brother to her: it was he she would call for on her deathbed, together with the prior of the Franciscans.

For Yourcenar Brussels was first and foremost the city where her mother died a few days after her birth. But Brussels was also the capital that first accepted her in its Academy, just as Liège was the first to open its university to her.

Yourcenar was enmeshed in a love-hate relationship with her native land – and had difficulty in separating both sentiments. The most reliable evidence for this is again her oeuvre: the grimy streets of Bruges; Bruges surrounded by fields and dunes; Bruges, a trap for Zeno, victim of the Inquisition; Bruges where he looks into the abyss, but to which he returns, even though he knows that his death sentence has been pronounced there.

An annual rainfall of 700 to 1,500 litres per square metre: Jacques Brel was hardly exaggerating when he sang of his flat home country, "with a sky so grey that it looks as if a canal has strung itself aloft". If in spite of everything Belgians are still cheerful, that is because they have learnt to look on the sunny side of things – which does not mean that they have forgotten how to battle against the elements.

The "man with the umbrella" who welcomes the visitor in Ter Hulpen's new museum, devoted to Jean-Michel Folon, perfectly typifies the state of mind of this graphic artist from Uccle, whose multicoloured birds have travelled round the world. Hergé always drew Thompson and Thomson holding umbrellas. And Tintin himself hardly ever leaves his dun-coloured raincoat behind. A garment we also meet on many other Belgian sleuths in detective stories or comic strips, such as, for instance, Commissioner Raffini. A master in portraying the dreariness of the rainy streets, Georges Simenon was never seen without his pipe and hat. Inspector Maigret followed his example . . .

So hats occupy a special place in the outward signs of being a Belgian. The most popular form of head-covering is still the cap – as the singer Jeff Bodart makes plain with fitting pride – but for a long time wearing a hat was a mark of respectability. Paul-Henri Spaak, the politician and a gifted orator, rarely appeared without this sartorial adornment. Casually worn, Magritte made it the universally present accessory for his "average man", his own double, who, seen from behind, features in his paintings. Ensor, when he immortalised himself in a self-portrait, wore a hat decorated with flowers and therefore less fitted to defy the rain. And the woman gracing the cigarette packets of the national Belga brand, where would she be without her wide-brimmed hat?

All this may explain why one day a young man from Liège conceived the idea of devoting his life to the milliner's art. By concentrating on quality, finish and materials, Elvis Pompilio made a serviceable article into a work of art. Today he has an international reputation. Every year he delivers more than twenty thousand original hats to his boutiques in Brussels, Antwerp, Paris and London, to the great delight of both the style-setters and dedicated hat lovers. Amélie Nothomb is one of them. This young writer, who, though she was born in Japan, is proud of her Belgian nationality, continues to amaze people with her novels. Yet now she is in her thirties her most striking feature is the almost unbelievable shapes of the hats she wears...

Frédéric Antoine

Amélie Nothomb
© Richard Dumas

Georges Simenon
Writer

AMSAB / © Keystone

Sex, writing and moving around were the main components in the life of Georges Simenon. He claimed to have slept with some 10,000 women, wrote more than 450 books, moved house about 27 times and lived in more than five countries. Simenon, born in 1903, grew up in a poor family in the grey industrial city of Liège. When he was 16 he went to work for a local paper. A few years later, keen to improve himself and having meanwhile married for the first time, he moved to Paris. There he discovered popular fiction, a genre that he soon made his own. He calculated that he could make plenty of money with this sort of book as long as he could write enough of them. And so he did: between 1923 and 1933 he wrote more than 200 popular novels under a variety of pseudonyms. The money rolled in and almost every evening Simenon painted the town red in the company of well-known figures such as Charlie Chaplin, Josephine Baker and Arthur Miller.

In 1929 he wrote his first Maigret story, the first of a series with which he will always be linked. Maigret, a middle-aged policeman, solved his cases by discovering the motive behind the crime. Simenon also wrote a large number of psychological novels. In these "serious novels" he unravelled the psyche of usually anguished protagonists who were at a turning point in their lives.

Writing was very hard on Simenon, physically and mentally. Before he started a new book, he had a medical examination. Then he wrote in a kind of trance, and following a strict routine: one chapter a day, seven to thirteen days per book and another day to read it through. Next the manuscript went to his publisher, and he went back to his doctor. Then he waited for the next attack of writing. Simenon's last book was in 1973. He spent his last years with his housekeeper to whom he dictated his memoirs. He died in 1989, as rich as he was controversial, in Lausanne in Switzerland.

The intellectual references and cultural infrastructure on which Belgian artists can orient themselves once they attain a certain level are not to be found primarily in their own country. That is certainly the case for literature, where French-speaking Belgians look towards Paris, Dutch-speakers towards Amsterdam. This is not so terrible; after all, Belgium is a small country and has the advantage that these artists are immediately immersed in an international context and obliged to develop broad mental horizons, which can only fertilise and enrich their work.

So, no, Hugo Claus is not a Dutch writer, nor are Suzanne Lilar, Conrad Detrez, Pierre Mertens, Jacqueline Harpman or Amélie Nothomb French. Even when they go and live abroad, most of them retain a pied-à-terre in Belgium or come back regularly. Even for the essayist Luc Sante, originating from Verviers, but who has lived in New York since his childhood, Belgium is a continuing reference. Jacques Brel may have become an international star, but he continued to worry in his songs about what he had left behind in Belgium.

Jacqueline Harpman
© Irmeli Jung

All of this is seldom merely a matter of sentimental attachment, but the result of a need for a context, which can manage without dominant trends, cliques or the introspection which is often characteristic of a large and powerful cultural area. The historically developed cultural rift resulted in no unequivocally "national" traditions coming into being. But, in its turn, this led to a cultural system which remained small scale and transparent. As a result, it was clear that, for example, established cultural organisations were susceptible to drastic modernisation, far more than would be the case abroad. This is how the rather rigid Koninklijke Muntschouwburg grew under Gerard Mortier's impulse and subsequently under Bernard Foccroule to become an international reference point for opera. The old-fashioned temple of culture, which the Munt had formerly been, acquired a cool and even sexy image as a result. Through the absence of a cultural power house and the accompanying officialdom a single line

Gerard Mortier
Festival Manager

© Wild&Team, Salzburg

Gerard Mortier gave new life to the world of opera by maligning it. During his years as a student he founded Jeugd-Opera (Youth Opera), an association which challenged the corniness and exclusivity of Flemish opera. After graduating in law and communication studies at the University of Ghent, this son of Ghent, born in 1944, was for a while joint programme organiser of the Festival of Flanders. He later worked as artistic director of the Dusseldorf opera, as director of the Frankfurt and Hamburg operas, as artistic director of Covent Garden, and until 1981 as technical adviser to the Paris Opera.

In the early 1980s he returned to Belgium and became director of the Muntschouwburg, the national opera. In ten years he breathed new life into the company. He attracted a new, young audience, but also built up an enormous mountain of debts. In 1990 he was tempted away by Salzburg to run the Festspiele there. Mortier had problems with this assignment in that it seemed primarily to be a cultural festival to dish up high culture to those who could pay for it. He wanted to transform Salzburg into a centre of cultural dynamism and innovation, and to make the festival accessible to everyone.

When in the summer of 2000 it became known that the extreme right-wing FPO party would take part in the Austrian government, he resigned. A little later he withdrew his resignation and promised to complete his contract and stay on until September 2001. Mortier sees himself as a kind of ambassador for tolerance, and makes no secret of his dislike of the extreme Right.

He still has one Festspiel to go, and then wants to spent a year studying in Berlin. Meanwhile he is keeping busy organising the new Forum for music and dance in Ghent, a grand and controversial project costing 2 billion francs. Mortier also wants to lecture at Ghent University on the relationship between theatre and politics.

of thinking in the Belgian world of culture is pretty unthinkable. Because of its nature the country gives at worst the appearance of cultural indifference, at best an intense and experienced liking for pluralism. This may explain why so many artists, from dancers, through writers and artistic organisers to comic strip designers, have no trouble taking their chances, even on an international platform. And conversely, why no small number of foreign artists come to live in Belgium because they experience the cultural climate as free and satisfying. That was already the case in the 19th century. Charles Baudelaire hid here from his creditors, Victor Hugo retained contact after his sojourn in Brussels with the publisher there who produced *Les Misérables*, Karl Marx wrote his Communist Manifesto there, Multatuli his *Max Havelaar*. It is striking that in recent years a whole colony of Dutch writers has settled in Belgium, including Benno Barnard, Gerard Reve, Oscar van den Boogaard and W. F. Hermans, who has since died. Brussels has even developed into an exceptionally good multicultural and even cosmopolitan centre for music and the performing arts.

In material terms, an artist would never have an easy time in Belgium, but the country simultaneously offers great tolerance and pluralism and therefore breathing space. This explains why, in a considerable number of works of art, in Brel's songs and in literature by Jacques De Decker or Koen Peeters, Belgium appears as an archetype, as the object of an ironic and even reversed patriotism, perhaps rather for what it is not than for what it actually is. Sometimes the sound of implicit nostalgia rings right through it, in the parodied longing for earlier – mythical – greatness, for instance, in the evocativeness of kings or of the 1958 Brussels World Exhibition. But this does not all have to be taken too seriously. The federal state, in the meantime stripped of its authority in cultural policy by state reforms, is in this regard only a metaphor for a place of freedom. Not more, but not less either.

Granadamedia © LWT

Hercule Poirot
Detective

Agatha Christie, the British author, made a Belgian detective the hero of her crime novels. It was partly an accident that he was Belgian, but so what! Hercule Poirot became known throughout the world as a detective who leaves nothing to chance. The character was first introduced in 1920 in Christie's maiden publication *The Mysterious Affair at Styles*. Poirot was immediately popular, although he cannot be called entirely likeable. He is too clever, pedantic, too much of a dandy and, as he says himself, not so much a detective, as *the* detective. The little man with his egg-shaped head, black moustache and bowler hat fascinated the public with his use of his "little grey cells." His trade mark is the quick solution of complicated crimes by noticing details that other people miss. The man is outstanding at his trade and knows it. It makes him a trifle smug. After his first appearance the retired Belgian detective solved crime after crime. A first collection of crime stories appeared in 1923; 32 more were to follow.

Agatha Christie (1890-1976) produced in all 79 novels and collections of short stories. In addition she wrote more than 12 plays, including *The Mousetrap*. Thanks to Hercule Poirot and her other creation, Miss Marple, Agatha Christie became the most famous crime writer in the world. About a billion books by her have been sold in English and another billion in more than 45 other languages. Only the Bible and Shakespeare surpass this. Poirot has been brought to life in cinema too, and his fans can also follow his exploits in a whole list of films and series on TV. In 1975, after 55 years of detective work, Poirot died, an old man, going senile, in *Curtain: Poirot's Last Case*. Poirot's death was a major news item: the detective even had an obituary on the front page of the *New York Times*.

Belgians: Only One of Each

Of course, it could also be proof of a liking for the small pleasures in life: in his house too, the Belgian lets you see that he enjoys the good life. Every Belgian wants his house to be spacious, with rooms that are sufficient in number, size and equipped with all the amenities. And, above all, he likes to see it as a form of self-expression. Because the Belgian's ultimate dream in life consists of building his own house, born as he is "with a brick in his stomach", the typical Belgian street does not necessarily create an attractive or harmonious impression, but it is certainly varied. No two houses are the same, not even when one is built on to the next.

But when he has to live in a tower block, packed in with others in uniform flats, the Belgian will start to die a little each day. Nevertheless, the large-scale building of collectively inspired flat complexes had its supporters, especially the modernist architect, Renaat Braem. He was of the opinion that the individualistic building aspirations of his residents made Belgium "the ugliest country in the world". But his idea that housing needed above all to be a machine for functional living (a view he had adopted from Le Corbusier, his admired master), never stood a chance.

When it comes to living, Belgians do not find a sense of well-being in strict functionality, but rather in the extent to which they can express their individuality, or, literally are given free rein to experience this individuality. Even if this comes out as kitsch architecture or a sloppy way of dealing with public space. The most talented architect has a tough time dealing with that desire for self-expression — and, for that matter, just as much trouble dealing with authorities who

want to regulate town and country planning. As far as that is concerned, even the Belgian authorities are the perfect reflection of the national spirit: only rarely do they give an innovative architectural stimulus. Furthermore, there is absolutely no lack of innovative architects – it is sufficient to name just a few, which include Bob Van Reeth, Luc Deleu, Charles Vandenhove, Lucien Kroll, Stéphane Beel, Jean Barthélémy, Hilde Daem, Paul Robbrecht, Jo Crepain and Pierre Arnould.

164

Equally, the lack of dominant traditions provides architects who have this sort of ambition a remarkable level of freedom. The fact that they often have to row against the tide of accepted opinion concerning architecture, provides them with great opportunity for creative freedom; it is no coincidence that two of the architects mentioned are also active in the plastic arts. Given the chance, they like to take it – and often exuberantly. Once again, problems can arise in fitting innovative architecture into the broader context, especially in towns, of course, many of which bear testimony to a rich architectonic past. Bob – who himself prefers the bOb style of writing his name – Van Reeth opted for a "light" way of fitting in his creations with a clear

Marc Corbiau, 1986 © Steven Brooke   **Bob Van Reeth, Roosmalen house at Antwerp** © Bastin & Evrard

geometric design, especially with a number of striking, sometimes daring realisations in Antwerp, including the Zuiderterras (South Terrace) and the Van Roosmalen house, for which he combined a tightly controlled volume with a façade section in an eye-catchingly powerful black and white motif. Charles Vandenhove, who tackled both the degenerate inner city of Liège, as well as designing large civic buildings, more specifically in the Netherlands, often reached into the past to embrace classical structures, such as pillars and pediments. He did not use them as fashionable post-modernist "citations", but with them endeavoured to restore basic architectural values, such as overall structure and accessibility, to their former place of honour.

In that identifiable, marked sense of individuality, a longing for self-expression is voiced on the one hand, whilst on the other it erupts from circumstantial pressure – although the two factors need not be mutually exclusive. If Belgians wanted to achieve something, irrespective of the field, they often had no other choice than to do it alone, they were on their own. One of the things that is striking is that Belgian sports people appear to excel more in individual sports than in team events.

André Jacqmain, Sart Tilman campus in Liège © Bastin & Evrard

Victor Horta
Architect

Victor Horta (1861-1947) first wanted to study music, but finally opted for architecture. He trained under Balat, the court architect and designer of the Royal Greenhouses in Laken, with classical patterns and materials, but with the addition of glass and iron. Victor Horta drew his inspiration from him, and went on to use glass and iron in domestic architecture.

In the early stages of his career he made a name for himself in Art Nouveau architecture. Horta broke away from the classical plan of the urban house, and developed it into a harmonious space bathed in light. He constructed his buildings with curving lines and forms which he derived from the world of vegetation. Horta thought that all the elements of a building should be in harmony with each other. For that reason he also paid great attention to small details: he would design a house from its walls down to the specifications for its furnishings. This method of working was extremely expensive and time consuming, which explains why he only designed a relatively small number of buildings. Best known are the Hotel Tassel and his own house, which is now a museum. In addition to middle-class houses, Horta also designed larger buildings, including the Socialist Maison du Peuple and Innovation, the Brussels department store.

After the First World War, Horta abandoned Art Nouveau and applied himself to Art Deco and neo-classicism, producing buildings in a more austere style, such as the Central Station and the Palais des Beaux Arts in Brussels. Although Horta had an international reputation as an architect even during his working life, he was not really recognised in his own country. To the great dismay of art lovers some of his masterpieces were mercilessly demolished during the 1960s, among them the Maison du Peuple. Times have changed, fortunately, and Horta is now recognised as an architect who breathed new life into architecture by using new materials and ideas. In the year 2000 UNESCO placed four of his houses on the World Heritage List.

Victor Horta, own house © 2001 - Bastin & Evrard/SOFAM - België

Tennis stars: Justine Hénin, Dominique Van Roost, Kim Clijsters,
Laurence Courtois, Els Callens © Isosport

Ulla Werbrouck and Gella Vandecaveye © Isosport

For example, whilst the national football team De Rode Duivels (The Red Devils) can attain
impressive scores in various tournaments, the real champions who reach the world top are to
be found in sports like tennis (with, if we confine ourselves to the younger generation, Sabine
Appelmans, Dominique Van Roost, Kim Clijsters, Justine Hénin and Els Callens), judo (Ulla
Werbrouck, Gella Vandecaveye), table-tennis (Jean-Michel Saive), motorcycling (Eric Geboers,
Joël Smets), athletics (Mohammed Mourhit) and swimming (Fred Deburghgraeve).

And then, of course, there is cycling. In the person of Eddy Merckx, this sport even provided the
country with its "Greatest Belgian of the 20th century". That tradition is continued today by
Johan Museeuw among others or, the most colourful member of the pack, Frank
Vandenbroucke. Both cyclists exhibit evidence of great pride in the commonplace background
from which they hail and combine it in a pretty spontaneous way with a well-developed sense
of self-awareness in terms of their sporting abilities, which can sometimes, unjustly, be confu-
sed with arrogance. Both allow themselves to be perceived as mavericks, individualists who like
nothing better than going their own way and who are not readily inclined to allow themselves
to be disciplined by team leaders, sponsors or organisers. Merckx, the archetypal sportsman,
testified to his versatility in just that stubbornness and individualistic passion in order to prove
himself. He did not limit himself to a single specialisation, but participated in competitions
throughout the entire season. He shone not only by winning with flying colours major compe-

Fred Deburghgraeve © Isosport

Jacky Ickx Archief Het Laatste Nieuws

titions divided into various stages like the Tour of France, Spain or Italy but also, for example, set the hourly record on the track, which for that matter he still retains today.

Cycling is based on a long tradition, which can trace its origins to the widespread use of the bicycle at the beginning of the 20th century. Way back then the so-called Flandriens made a name for themselves in epics such as the Tour of France. These *coureurs* – Romain Maes, Sylveer Maes, Briek Schotte and many others – developed into real national heroes who made spectacular achievements in what were often rigorous and unrewarding circumstances, which would nowadays appear ridiculously primitive. These were racers who, as it were, operated from their back parlour or the shed at the bottom of the garden. They did it on their own, in the beginning were unable to live on the proceeds and were supported only by a few understanding members of their family. They were fired by the ambition to show that they were the best and needed that stubbornness, hard work and perseverance. They did it "by character" since personal willpower was often the only "capital" they had to invest in order to achieve their goal.

Afzien (to have a tough time) is a Flemish word which, via cycling, has become internationally recognised. Their modest background also resulted in their not feeling too good about, quite

Eddy Merckx
Cyclist

© Isosport

When in the year 2000 the Belgian media were looking for the "Belgian of the century' they were fairly unanimous in choosing the cyclist Eddy Merckx. Worshipped by all Belgians, respected by the cycling world, it is impossible to describe him without superlatives. This man is without question a Belgian icon. It is very dangerous to pick out anyone in a branch of sport as the best ever, but in cycling you can. Merckx, born in 1945, had by the time he was 28 already set more records than any other cyclist before him. His list of wins includes five Tours, five Giros, one Vuelta, one Tour of Switzerland, three times Paris-Nice, seven times Milan-San Remo, five times Liège-Bastogne-Liège. On top of that he has won three world titles, a national tricolour, broken the one-hour world record, been "Belgian Sportsman of the Year" six times, and "World Sportsman of the Year" three times. His enormous hunger for victory earned him the nickname "The Cannibal".

Merckx's career was characterised by his immense versatility; he achieved his wins over very different types of terrain. A good example of this is his win in the 1969 Tour de France, when he went home with the yellow jersey (overall winner), the green jersey (Best Sprinter) and the Best-Climber jersey in his possession. Moreover, he was very tough. In contrast to the current trend, he was at his peak for the whole cycling season, from March to October. As a cyclist Merckx was a rather withdrawn man, who thought only of cycling. Because cycling dominated his life, people often only knew the introvert cyclist, though outside the circuit he was a jovial man who liked to enjoy himself.

The greatest cyclist of all times retired from competitive cycling in 1979 and opened a bicycle factory near Brussels. He now follows cycle competitions from a distance. However, his only son Axel is also a cyclist. When in the summer of 2000 he became the Belgian Road Champion, Eddy awaited him at the finishing line with tears of pride.

Mohammed Mourhit
© Isosport

Sport in Belgium: the loneliness of the long-distance runner

Another Belgian characteristic is undoubtedly their sense of individualism. Everyone does their own thing, everyone owns their own house. It takes time here before the family capital is split up, or a real research team is assembled at the university. It is far more in the Belgian nature to battle on alone. As in academia, so in sport. Belgians, of course, do like the collective sport of football, but the country's really 'great' sports stars are usually loners.

As the five-times winner of the Tour de France, the 'Belgian Sportsman of the Century', Eddy Merckx, was never more magnificent than when he broke away by himself in the mountains, or when he made his solitary attempt on the one-hour world record. Rik Van Steenbergen and Rik Van Looy, his illustrious predecessors, already had some of this fighting spirit. The same can be said of the 'kleine klimmer', the little climber, Lucien Van Imper, and of yet other champions who succeeded Merckx.

Judo, another sport in which Belgium shines, is marked by the same individualism.

Gella Vandecaveye and Ulla Werbrouck followed in the footsteps of Ingrid Berghmans, the 'Belgian Sportswoman of the Century'. We find this 'battling with oneself' again: in tennis – in spite of sometimes playing doubles – with Dominique Monami-Van Roost and Sabine Appelmans (and in the 1950s, the famous Washer-Brichant partnership); in table-tennis with Jean-Michel Saive; and in swimming with Frederik Deburghgraeve, Brigitte Becue and Carine Verbauwen.

The chosen terrain of the lone struggle is, however, athletics. No wonder that Belgians have distinguished themselves there, in the five thousand and ten thousand metres and in the marathon: from the times of Gaston Reiff until now with Mohammed Mourhit, via Gaston Roelants, Emile Puttemans, Karel Lismont and Ivo Van Damme, who died far too young and pointlessly.

Frédéric Antoine

literally, getting dirty. In the muddy ground of cycling this earned them a handsome record of achievements, nowadays with Sven Nys or Erwin Vervecken. In more sophisticated sports like motor racing, which requires sizeable investment and infrastructure and which uses up a great deal of money, Belgians are, in contrast, a lot less conspicuous, except in bygone days with the isolated examples of Jacky Ickx or Thierry Boutsen.

Many Belgian "success stories" are based on the triumph of individuality and personal perseverance — although this is often clearly by necessity, since the small-scale beginning is frequently rooted in incomprehension and indifference. This is even the case on an economic and industrial level. The creative stimulus in that sector seldom started from large, established enterprises or from the major holdings who were a little too fond of taking a tight hold on their real monopolies. Venture capital has never been easy to come by in Belgium. The "people with an idea" mostly work their way to the fore from a modest background, from surroundings where a human scale still exists and individual ambition and creativity are not curbed by bureaucracy, conservatism or nervous shareholders. It is not for nothing that Belgium has generated so few multinationals: economic growth is supported by the innovative potential of the SMEs — smal and medium — sized companies. If it is an indication: if the growth of previous years has also improved employment opportunities it was not thanks to the large companies — on the contrary — but to SMEs.

The "garages of Silicon Valley", where the computer revolution was born of enterprising young amateurs originally working in isolation, have always existed in Belgium. Because not it was so much the established laboratories but just those garages (or their equivalent) that were clearly the real breeding ground. Lieven Gevaert with his photographic paper or Paul Janssen with his pharmaceutical products, to name but two, emerged in this way. Both Gevaert — who was allied with the German Agfa for many years — and Janssen Pharmaceutica — now part of an American multinational — developed in their sector to become world players. In the same way as the cash point machine was invented, Georges Lemaître, now as good as forgotten, discovered the Big Bang theory, Marc van Montagu and Walter Fiers, from an unpretentious laboratory in Ghent, collaborated on the basis of genetic manipulation. A somewhat exceptional example, but valuable as an illustration, is the case of Jo Lernout and Pol Hauspie, in Belgium the great inventors and promoters of speech technology. They kept their activity very regional, close to their back door as it were, even though their expansion had reached the United States and the Far East. They experienced enormous problems in convincing financial backers, had to invest more time in the search for funding than in developing their technology, which tempted them to stray off the regular road into some "creative" bookkeeping, which finally led their enterprise into serious problems.

The result of all of this is that invention and innovation are, to a large extent, closely associated with the individuals who may demand the first income for their endeavours. Even in the arts that same phenomenon arises. Of course, the basis of artistic creativity is almost always extremely individual. Nevertheless, it is noticeable that artistic "teamwork" can very

Laurent Busine
© Belga

Plan K at Charleroi
© Pino Pipitone

Rosas: Drumming © Herman Sorgeloos

Alain Platel and Les Ballets C de la B: *lets op Bach* © Chris Va

often be personified. In classical music celebrated orchestras are always associated with the names of their founders, conductors and artistic directors, like Philippe Herreweghe, Paul Van Nevel, Sigiswald Kuyken and Jan Caeyers. The most dynamic modern art museums are never talked about without the mention of their driving force, Laurent Busine in Charleroi and Jan Hoet in Ghent. Contemporary dance always evokes the names of Anne Teresa de Keersmaecker, Wim Vandekeybus and Alain Platel. For them the classical notion of "ballet" is hardly appropriate, for a number of reasons, including the fact that in their relative isolation they could scarcely find a link with existing tradition. As a result they acquired considerable freedom, which led to their being able to give important new stimulus to modern-day performing arts, specifically by integrating, in an organic way, dance, music, theatre, art and literature. With their companies, respectively Rosas, Ultima Vez and Le Ballets C. de la B., they attained, just like Jan Fabre, (who is principally engaged in the plastic arts) wide international recognition.

That individuality is, in many ways, both a curse and a blessing. Brilliant ideas, because of the enforced small-scale of their creation, have not always received the support and framework they deserved. It is even possible that potential talent is nipped in the bud because the required related conditions for further evolution were lacking. But individualism, whether personally chosen or not, has certainly shielded numerous other developments from the suffocating conformity that is inherent in organisation, regulation, tradition and large-scale

connections. And that last one is, by definition, the first condition to enable creativity to blossom. If only there is a fool with sufficient single-mindedness and willpower to take the creativity within him seriously.

Contemporary Dance or "The Belgian Wave"?

In the early 1980s Belgium became an important place on the world map of contemporary dance. Until then classical ballet had been predominant, in the form of the Royal Flanders Ballet, the Royal Walloon Ballet and Maurice Béjart's Ballet of the XXth century. The resounding international success of a few young choreographers changed all that. Anne Teresa De Keersmaeker scored high points with Fase *(1982) and* Rosas danst Rosas *(1983). Jan Fabre made his name with* De macht der theaterlijke dwaasheden *(1984) and* De Danssecties *(1987) and Wim Vandekeybus had the*

audience in the palm of his hand with What The Body Does Not Remember *(1987).*

Soon everyone was talking about the "Belgian Wave" as if it were a large, concerted dance movement. However, the only thing De Keersmaeker, Fabre and Vandekeybus had in common was their context. They could not look for great examples, well-trained dancers or an extensive dance circuit in Belgium. So they had to get their inspiration from international dance and theatre practice, and mould it to their own will without scruple. And they were

Famous and Memorable Belgians. These too are Belgians

all so typically Belgian that they could only do their work thanks to non-Belgian dancers and financial support from abroad.

But Belgium soon made up the lost ground. At once several talented organisers raised their heads in Flanders, the art centres offered a platform for this new talent and there was strong lobbying to get a good system of subsidies off the ground. In the mid-1990s the gap in dance education was also filled by PARTS.

In Francophone Belgium, where people like Nicole Moussoux, Patrick Bonté, Pierre Droulers and Michèle Ann De Mey had been building a reputation for years, the great step was taken in 1990 by simply abolishing the Royal Walloon Ballet. This immediately meant the foundation of Charleroi/Danses, Centre Chorégraphique de la Communauté française de Belgique. Frédéric Flamand became the artistic director, and found himself not only with a large dance company under his wing, but also responsibility for the rest of the Francophone choreographers.

In Flanders, meanwhile, the heroes of the 1980s continued to do well. There was, however, no artistic succession. Alain Platel joined the club a few years later, but after that there was a ghastly silence. An obvious reason to welcome the American Meg Stuart with open arms as a Belgian choreographer.

In recent years it has been the graduates of PARTS in particular who continue to enrich Belgian dance. Attracted by Belgium's reputation for dance, they come from all over the world. After their training here they surprisingly often "hang on" and they find, together with some fellow students, the backing to realise their first projects and a public that waits for them with bated breath. And wondering whether their work is now more Belgian or less so, more or less of a wave then that of the 1980s stars . . .

Dominike Van Besien
Senior Editor with Radio Clara, dance critic

Jan Hoet
Museum Director

Jan Hoet almost acquired the doubtful honour of having been a curator without a museum for 25 years. However, in 1999 the eccentric Hoet finally acquired his own exhibition space. He virtually lives in his museum and if his wife did not ring him up at lunch time, he would forget to eat.

Jan Hoet was born in Louvain in 1936 to an art-loving family who moved to Ghent some ten years later. After a career in education, he was appointed curator of the new Museum of Contemporary Art in Ghent in 1975. He was not discouraged by the fact that the museum did not have its own building. Over the years he assembled an impressive collection of modern art and organised a series of important exhibitions. In 1986 he first came into the limelight of the world press with his Chambres d'amis project, in which art was displayed in 51 private homes. His career reached a peak in 1992, when he was given the contract to direct Documenta 9, the international art exhibition in Kassel in Germany.

Hoet does not shun the media. It is obvious to him that the media and new technology are involved in art and the dissemination of art. At the opening of his Municipal Museum For Contemporary Art (SMAK – Stedelijk Museum voor Actuele Kunst) he therefore pulled out all the stops: he himself had a boxing match with an artist, a whole flock of artists performed, and the evening finished with a techno-party. Publicity was assured. In 2000 he organised Over the Edges, the most talked-of exhibition of the year. Artists had their work displayed all over the city of Ghent, so that it became part of the city landscape. Hoet had again brought art to the people, just as he introduced several artists, including Panamarenko, to the general public.

Jan Hoet is now approaching retirement age, but is still as active as ever. He is extending a museum in Herford in Germany, and is adviser to various other artistic projects outside Belgium. Moreover, on 1 July 2001 he will succeed himself as artistic director of SMAK, but no longer as a permanent employee of the City of Ghent.

The World Is An Image

The best known painting by the best known Belgian artist depicts nothing other than a bold-ly brushed everyday item: a pipe. It was painted by René Magritte and has, over the years, grown into an icon. Yet the painting "exists" only because of the short sentence written under-neath, which claims that there is no pipe involved here. The image can imitate reality but not replace it. But also: nothing is what it appears to be, behind the visible world another lies hid-den. Consequently, *ceci n'est pas une pipe*, although at first sight it would certainly appear to be one.

Magritte's painting bears witness to a questioning, reflective association with the image. Not that Magritte was attempting to define the limits of pictorial potential nor put it into perspective by pointing out the supremacy of "genuine" reality. On the contrary, he was trying with his paintings to explore the uncharted possibilities of the image. Mostly starting from an unorthodox assembly of the very familiar, often commonplace or even banal elements, occasionally supported with text, he showed in his work that the artistic image can sometimes generate loudly proclaimed new significance. Belief in this literally subversive power of art explains, apart from that, why surrealism, the style that flourished in the 1920s in Francophone

René Magritte,
The intimate friend, 1958
© Sabam

René Magritte
Surrealist Painter and Theoretician

Middle-class men with bowler hats, a pipe, white clouds in a blue sky – these are only a few of the images directly associated with René Magritte. The surrealist François Ghislain Magritte was born in 1889 in Lessines. He started his career as a designer of wallpaper and advertising material, and painted in his free time. He soon became intrigued by the absurd and paradoxical, and experimented with Futurism and Cubism. Magritte was looking for a style of his own and, influenced by his advertising work, assimilated its imagery and words into his paintings. In his art he raised questions about everyday things, by showing them in unconventional ways.

In 1927 he had his first one-man exhibition, and he gradually became known as a surrealist. That same year Magritte moved to Paris to work with the French surrealists, but three years later he returned permanently to Brussels. In 1930 he produced one of his best-known works, a picture of a pipe with the caption below: *Ceci n'est pas une pipe* (This is not a pipe). With this painting he wanted to focus attention on the difference between an object and the two-dimensional representation of it. From 1948 his collaboration with a New York art dealer brought him renown internationally. Magritte went on painting until his death, always in a corner of his sitting room, surrounded by newspapers.

He died in Schaarbeek in 1967, one of the greatest Belgian artists of the 20th century. On the death of his widow, some 20 years later, there were problems: she had made no arrangements for the disposal of his unsold paintings, so that they were put up for auction and scattered over the whole world, much to the displeasure of many art lovers. After all these years, Magritte's paintings have still not lost their originality and the painter is known and much in demand, not only by art lovers but by the general public, an aspect which the advertising industry gratefully takes advantage of.

James Ensor,
Pierrot et squelettes, 1907
© SABAM

Jan Fabre, The man who measures the clouds
© SABAM / Photo: Bart Lasuy

Belgium, in the expressive arts as well as literature, photography and music, became strongly linked with the political left. Just as in French surrealism, the most radical representatives of it in Belgium, resolutely opted for communism .

Belgian art in the first decades of the 20th century revealed its great sensitivity for foreign avant-garde, such as German expressionism, Dada and therefore for French surrealism. Those specific influences were all linked with a critical, essentially ambiguous relationship with the image, with the intention of evoking a deeper, hidden reality against the accepted middle class and academic norms. This Belgian artistic sensitivity to modernistic influences was not built on coincidence nor did it spring purely from copying what was fashionable. The enrichment which the often ironical works of Magritte or the more aesthetic paintings of Paul Delvaux had to offer international (and also internationally inspired) surrealism, is also too important for that.

Their work continues a centuries-old, pictorial tradition, of which the origins were born in the Middle Ages with the Flemish Primitives. This tradition bore witness from the earliest days, in the phantasmagorical paintings of the late 15th, early 16th-century paintings of Hieronymus Bosch, to an explicit inclination for reflection. In his hands, the image was able to enjoy emancipation away from the established religious or middle class artistic conventions of the time. As a result, these works created space for the frenzied, for the exploration of myste-

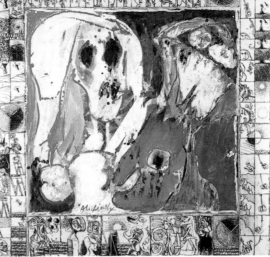

Wim Delvoye , Wedgewood I
© Wim Delvoye

Alechinsky
La jeune fille et la mort, 1966-1967
© SABAM

ries, of dreams and anxieties. This tendency towards expressive inventiveness was continued by Rubens, who was especially interested in the social elite, and certainly Breughel who, with his compassionate view of earthly display, concentrated his attention strikingly often on the everyday lifestyle of common people.

An often-proposed theory suggests that this pictorial tradition strengthened the link with the political and cultural context in which it developed. The supposition originates from the Southern Netherlands, which was predominantly Catholic, the region which, in broad terms, later became Belgium. Catholicism fostered a great mistrust of the Word for a very long time. It forbade the personal, individual reading of the Bible, albeit the Book of Books, even though literacy had progressed so little at that time. That wariness towards language and writing increased with the Counter-Reformation and its closely associated, general climate of repression and censure at the time of the Catholic and Spanish domination in Early New Age, when there was scarcely any mention of freedom of thought. Other than in the "free" Protestant North, the pictorial, drawing and painting, remained the only more or less "safe" outlet for artistic expression and critical reflection. The medium was able to fulfil this role because it was much more difficult for those in power to identify and check for conformity, although, of course, the artists needed to seek cover in ambivalence and disguise. But that simultaneously obliged them to pursue their craft just as critically, more precisely, to draw out all its potential.

Famous and Memorable Belgians. These too are Belgians

This early history created an artistic sensitivity which produced a receptive attitude towards modernistic innovation and insight. If Bosch can be used to situate the source, then Magritte is the 20th-century reference point. Many Belgian artists today consider themselves, with good reason, as "Magritte's children". But they were unable to become just that without undergoing the influence of the next high point in this pictorial tradition. This occurred in the 1960s and 1970s with Marcel Broodthaers. In his work, which principally consists of installations and banal objects, like eggshells and mussel shells, became the symbols of the obedient, narrow-minded lifestyle, a place in collages and all kinds of collections which brought them a new context and with it a new significance. Its quiet poetry found its counterpart in the work in which Broodthaers revealed an extremely critical view of artistic practice and developed a radical political and ideological vision which ran throughout his work.

Broodthaers' poetic aspirations found a parallel and a continuation in Panamarenko's meticulously fabricated, apparently "real" objects. His aeroplanes, mechanical chickens and submarines are produced with great technical precision but were never intended to "really" function, although they gave that impression. As a result, they exert a provocative force on the functional pretensions of technique and economics, whilst in all their supposed uselessness they simultaneously provide a poetic comment. This same artistic approach is noticeable in many Belgian artists: the allusion to the everyday and, in general, to objects or disciplines, like science and technique, which do not match aesthetic conformity. With some artists, just because of that, an occasionally poetic, sometimes alienating effect that not only highlights problems in the world but also in practising art exists. These include Guillaume Bijl, Patrick Corillon, Michel François, Jan Fabre and Wim Delvoye. Their work bears witness to that same "pictoriality" which is not so much beautiful but attempts to be light-hearted, critical and put things into perspective.

The extroversion within this expressive tradition explains why, as soon as it got the chance, it looked for a niche in the mass media. It attained its greatest blossoming in the comic strip, which developed more specifically in newspapers. Although the comic strip was original-

top: Marcel Broodthaers, Pot of
SMAK © Dirk
bottom: Panamarenko, Scotch
Ludion / © Panamarenko © Photo: D.V

ly considered to have a purely entertainment function, and was intended primarily for children, almost at once a committed and satirical tone crept in. That was already the case with the forefather of the modern Belgian comic strip, Hergé, who brought his legendary hero Tintin into the world in 1929. He sent immediately him to the Soviet Union so that he could, admittedly from a reactionary Catholic point of view, denounce dictatorship and repression. Here too the realistic impression predominated. Hergé's "clear line" style was intended to be transparent so that throughout the visual familiarity an equally clear and familiar, complete message could be delivered.

After the Second World War a real "Belgian school" came into being in weekly comic strips like Spirou and Fantasio and Tintin, intended for young people, and, principally on the Flemish side, in the daily press. They served to take up the cause against the massive import of cheaply delivered cartoons from the United States. The fact that Belgian cartoonists won the battle testifies that, with their own style, they could match the expectations of their readership. A combination of adventure and humour was clearly the formula for success for cartoonists such as, to name but a few, Franquin, (Spirou and Fantasio, Gaston Lagaffe), Willy Vandersteen (Willy and Wanda also known as Bob and Bobette and currently as Spike and Suzy), Morris (Lucky Luke), Peyo (The Smurfs) and Marc Sleen (Nero). One-dimensional heroes have been created by Belgian comic strip designers to a much lesser extent with the exception of, for example, E. P. Jacobs (Blake and Mortimer), who made an impact with his epic breadth and the elaborated monumentality of his drawings, which can be recognised once more in the architecturally influenced style of François Schuiten, among others. In parallel with the comic strip the cartoonists formed their own family tree , with the major contemporary offshoots being Royer, Gal and Zak, with a younger generation making its presence felt in a number of small and less small publications. Some of them, with their derisive or satirical view of the world, have achieved great success abroad, such as Quirit in the Netherlands, Kamagurka in France and the Netherlands and Benoît in the United States.

A major segment of the post-war Belgian comic strip developed from the – as short-lived as it was unsuccessful and, as a result, also barely known – plan from the 1944-45 years, to create from the ground up a local cartoon industry modelled on the American Disney

Tintin
Comic Strip Hero

A reporter without ever having to write, years of experience without getting any older, countless friends, but never a girlfriend … that must be Tintin. The comic strip hero with his quiff is a reporter who can't sit still: his first adventure took him straight to the Soviet Union, and later he travelled the whole world in the 24 albums drawn by his spiritual father, Hergé. As a reporter he did not really make the grade: he wrote almost nothing! Hergé constantly made his hero have politically coloured adventures, but in spite of that the reporter has an enormous attraction for readers all over the world. This is because Tintin is a naïve individual without clear features, personality or age. For this reason everyone, young or old, whatever their political convictions, can identify with him. Round this flat personality Hergé created a galaxy of colourful characters. The hot-tempered Captain Haddock is the first to come to mind, but there is also the absent-minded Professor Calculus, and the extremely incompetent detectives Thomson and Thompson are rewarding creations.

Hergé, whose real name is Georges Remi, was editor of Le Petit Vingtième, the children's supplement of the conservative Catholic newspaper *Le Vingtième Siècle*, when on 10 January 1929 he first brought Tintin and Snowy to life. Hergé drew in a very clear style and with a keen eye for detail. The style became known as "clear line", and was to have a great influence both on Hergé's contemporaries and on later generations of cartoon artists. After the comic books came a weekly cartoon magazine, TV series, stamps, statuettes … Tintin-mania was born. The artist died in 1983, and the last unfinished album, *Tintin and Alpha Art*, was published posthumously. It was Hergé's wish that no successor should be appointed, so that his death would also mean the end of his hero's adventures. That does not mean that Tintin has disappeared with him – to the contrary. The decision to dedicate one of the restored spheres of Atomium to Tintin puts him back into the spotlight and brings two of Belgium's icons together.

Robbedoes by Franquin
© Dupuis

Lucky Luke
© Morris 2001

The Miracle of The Belgian Comic Strip

The international success of Tintin, Blake and Mortimer, the Smurfs and Lucky Luke defies debate. It is simply a fact. Nevertheless, it remains an amazing phenomenon. How did a small country like Belgium manage to create so many mythical series in the world of the Ninth Art? Closer examination reveals that it is just because of our country's small size that so much talent has devoted itself to the comic strip. Originally, Franquin, Morris and Peyo were aiming for a career as producers of cartoon films. But when the Disney studios started their madcap ride, steamrollering the small Belgian studios out of existence, these budding young artists, who did not fancy moving to Hollywood, sought refuge in children's comics, Spirou and Fantasio and Tintin. Thanks to its limited market, Belgium escaped the strict scrutiny of the censor boards in France. The comic strip was scarcely taken

seriously there, so the devotees of the strip could allow their imagination free rein. This climate of freedom in our country also attracted French writers: Jacques Martin, Jean Graton and, not to be forgotten, the famous duo Goscinny-Uderzo developed their style in Belgian magazines. Unforgettable characters were born in Belgium: Tintin, of course, but also Alex, Blake and Mortimer, Spirou and Fantasio, Gaston Lagaffe, Boule and Bill. Even though most of them are in their 50s now, they nevertheless still remain of unchanging value in the world of publishing.

The golden age of the Belgian comic strip, between 1950 and 1970, had a less favourable corollary. The generation who had to succeed the Franquins and Peyos of this world, often stepped apparently paralysed through the prestigious legacy, into the trap of the shy, *characterless copy. From the 1970s we remember especially the birth of the adult comic strip in France with Pilote, started by Goscinny and his Belgian collaborator, the great scriptwriter, Jean-Michel Charlier.*

During the 1990s the major Belgian publishers were swallowed up by large European groups: Lombard passed into the hands of Dargaud, Casterman was taken over by Flammarion, and the Dupuis family sold its patrimony to the businessman Albert Frère. From an economic point of view, the Belgian comic strip became a French-Belgian enterprise. But, once again, it was the stars made in Belgium who dominated the galaxy: the Brussels scriptwriter Jean Van Hamme became the Midas of the classic adventure

comic strips, with best-seller series such as XIII and Largo Winch. Behind this one substantial tree a whole wood of new writers lies in wait: people like Stassan, Bodart, Lapière and Frank Pé and, in the north of the country and with a completely different tone, Schallaert, Bosschaert and Cromheecke. They prove that Belgium, even if the illustrious time of the weekly rivalry between Tintin and Spirou and Fantasio in the comics has gone forever, remains an impressively fertile breeding ground for talent. Our little country has not yet had the last word in the world of the text balloons...

Hugues Dayez
Radio journalist for RTBF

Studios. Not so much the lack of success – with Belvision as one of the few exceptions to this – as the ambition is important here: the desire to carry the pictorial tradition forward into the more or less new medium of the period, film. The small domestic market and the associated modesty of available financial means led to Belgian film remaining close to reality. It developed its own visual language for its topics, sometimes socially critical and sometimes ironic in tone which, both from choice as well as (financial) necessity distances itself from the standard Hollywood clichés.

Another episode was within reach: television. Belgian television had invested for some time in often much respected young people's programmes. Aimed at young children, equally educational as relaxing, Flemish television's TikTak enjoyed world-wide success. The

The Smurfs
Happy Blue Woodland Creatures

© IMPS

The most famous inhabitants of the woods are not dwarfs or elves. They are Smurfs, the cartoon figures created by Peyo (1928-1992). The average Smurf is three apples high, bright blue, has a big fat nose and wears white trousers and a white hat. As well as ordinary Smurfs, there are Very Important Smurfs, such as the wizard Papa Smurf, recognisable by his red trousers, Brainy, Jokey and, oddly enough, only one female Smurf, Smurfette. In recent years there have in addition been a few baby Smurfs, who apparently are found at certain times of the year underneath plants. Every Smurf has its own qualities and faults, but together they form a happy, rather egalitarian community where it's nice to be. The Smurfs live at peace with the animals in the woods and have only one great enemy, the sorcerer, Gargamel, who with his cat, Azrael, hunts them down to use them in his magic potions.

Peyo, who was really Pierre Culliford, created the Smurfs in 1958. Originally they were secondary figures in his Johan and Peewit comic strip, but the blue creatures soon became stars with their own adventures. The series always dealt with easily identifiable subjects: friendship, jealousy, or the age-old struggle between good and evil. After the comic strip came the television series in which the Smurfs' adventures became extremely popular in, among other places, America. The signature song of the series, the "la la la" song, became a widely recognised tune. The characters lend themselves extremely well to merchandising and Smurf products are collected by young and old. Soon the Smurfs, *los pitufos, les schtroumpfs* and *i puffi* became household words. In France they even built a Smurf amusement park. The Smurfs have also had an influence on language: in 'Smurf' the most important words in a sentence are replaced by the word 'smurf' or a derivative of it. That language is now understood by everyone and smurfed by grownups as well as children.

public broadcasting system in Francophone Belgium proved to be a veritable breeding ground for young, inventive and often emotionally-committed makers of documentaries. In Flanders, the liberalisation of the broadcasting system enabled local television production to flourish. The production company Woestijnvis set the style with popular but intelligent and not in the least populist entertainment programmes. It succeeded in exporting several of its ideas; its formula for the soap thriller De Mol (The Mole) was sold to dozens of countries.

I Am Going To Make A Guess, Walter... Woestijnvis!

You must admit, it isn't nice to be confronted almost daily with a blunder from your past. Suppose, more than ten years ago, as a likeable chap from West Flanders, you took part in the Flemish version of the popular TV game Wheel of Fortune. You are just a fraction away from the end. And then comes the crunch and you hear yourself saying: "I am going to make a guess, Walter. The animal we are looking for is a woestijnvis (desert fish)!"

General merriment in the studio and later in all Flemish living rooms. Rommel, the Desert Fox (Woestijnvos), turned in his grave. And when after many years this bloomer slides from the collective memory, and you can again go about your life as a respected citizen,

you are nailed to your pillory again by some creative television people, because precisely this lapse is the name chosen for a new Flemish production company.

Yet the unlucky candidate can also be rather proud, since Woestijnvis very quickly became the most successful production company in Flanders. With programmes such as Man bijt Hond (Man Bites Dog), De xii Werken (The Twelve Works) and De Mol (The Mole) it has even been responsible for the revival of public service broadcasting in Flanders, which in 1996 was on the verge of death. "VRT (Flemish Broadcasting Service) is an ugly old lady, but we very much like to watch her." is how Wouter Vandenhaute, head of Woestijnvis, explains the intense relationship with his foster mother.

Not that he is worried by an Oedipus complex, since his extramarital sidelines are becoming more numerous. In Flanders he remains faithful to VRT, but once over the borders he pops into bed with more and more partners. And he is not embarrassed. He even leaves his business card behind, so that we see the name Woestijnvis appearing on ever more foreign television screens, together with the umpteenth clone of his prettiest child, De Mol; the hugely popular thriller soap which has

already been sold in 46 different countries.

In Flanders, however, Woestijnvis has not been "that nice little production company" for a long time now. Here you are generally popular if you come up from nothing and launch a direct hit. But if you manage to make the occasional successful programme for four years running, then there is something wrong and the wind changes automatically. Vultures look expectantly for the day Woestijnvis bites the dust. While they wait they accuse the creative Flemish gang of "money-grabbing practices with government money", and the little "boss" with his "crew cut" is proclaimed one of the most powerful media personalities in the country. "It is easy to make good television this way,"' you hear more and more often. And so people would rather see hundreds of millions flow to the Dutch television giant Endemol for the elevating spectacle of Big Brother. Certainly now that the Zaventem "mafia" are also daring to disrupt the readers' market with their new super journal: Bonanza.

Leo Bonte

Freelance Journalist with daily De Standaard

Laughing is Serious Business

Belgium is, historically speaking, a country which, certainly culturally, is dominated by the petite bourgeoisie – or in present-day sociological terms, by the middle class. More than farmers, who are tied to the ground, countryside and animals, or labourers, who have to go along with the boss and labour regulations, the petite bourgeoisie exhibit an inclination for gentle anarchy. They clearly have a difficult time accepting rules, especially when they are imposed by the authorities. In its nastier aspects this leads to a lack of social discipline, for example in traffic or towards the tax man. On the positive side of these habits, noteworthy are the lack of hollow formalism, a gift for self-mockery and an instinct for freedom.

As a result, not very many purely "classical" heroes feature in the Belgian comic strip. They are mostly ordinary little men who did not choose to be in the adventures they experience but were rather dropped into them by coincidence. And they all have deficiencies or failings. Peyo's Smurfs are finally just runts, Franquin's Gaston Lagaffe is exactly what his name suggests: a clumsy bungler. The most popular among the comic strip characters are just those dented heroes, or more often, second-class figures. Not Tintin but his companion Captain Haddock, for example, who would be willing to submit for a sip of Loch Lomond, or the detectives Thomson and Thompson, who always end up in seven ditches at the same time. Not Willy and Wanda, otherwise known as Bob and Bobette, and currently as Spike and Suzy, but the rather gawky and vain Lambik or Orville, currently Ambrose. Cowboy Henk, the creation of Kamagurka and Herr Seele, is constantly – admittedly always full of beans; a victim of his monomania, just as

Philippe Geluck's Cat is just a little fatter and more obstinate than can really be good for him.

This bunch of characters provides the laughs. And Belgians like laughing, especially at themselves. In fact, they would be the first to call themselves "little Belgians" and to recognise themselves in caricatures, although they would not necessarily immediately appreciate that coming from outsiders. But Flemish commercial television bristles with programmes where the text material consists almost entirely of jokes, in which Antwerp residents, Limburgers and West Flemings, sometimes in coarse stereotypes, constantly poke fun at each other. It appears never to become boring.

The tendency to put things in perspective remains, somehow or other, to be a source of healthy humour, which does not fight shy of highlights that come close to absurdity. The Brussels word *zwans* (jest) is the best word for it, although for sure it is a term which is almost impossible to translate. Entertainers and variety artists like Annie Cordy and Urbanus owe their success to it, in France and the Netherlands respectively. The ironic style, which is noticeable in both literature and sculpture, can be traced back to the same source. Much has to do with a penchant for detachment and a certain incapacity for seriousness, which at the same time opens up the willingness to accept nothing as indisputable and to look at everything from all sides at the same time, with a view to discovering its comic aspect.

Annie Cordy
Entertainer

Annie Cordy never had any particular ambition to enter the world of show business. It was only because she was so thin that her mother sent her to dancing classes, to strengthen her up a bit. Annie, born Léonie Cooreman in 1928, had talent and her dancing teacher immediately spotted that. With his encouragement she also took singing lessons and entered cabaret contests. Annie proved to be a born variety artist and in 1949 won a major cabaret prize. In the audience was a talent scout who helped her find a job at the famous Paris Lido. Annie was not interested in the glamour and glitter. She preferred to present her songs sincerely and straightforwardly, and with unbridled energy, just like herself. From the Lido she went to the Moulin Rouge, where her show was again a great success. The fashion for intellectual chanson, aimed at a wide audience, was at its peak. Annie's performances were just what people wanted to see and hear.

She was carried off to America, where they would almost not let her go again. Rio, Cuba, Mexico, New York, everywhere they fell at her feet. Her shows were just as popular in the other half of the world: she played to full houses in Russia too.

Annie Cordy scored one hit after another and became a star in the true sense of the word. But a singing career was apparently not enough. She started acting. Throughout her career she sparkled on the silver screen, but also in TV series and on the boards. She appeared in more than 30 films, some 20 television series and a dozen stage plays. In between her stage and film work she continued to sing and do live performances. During her career she recorded more than 500 songs, and most people can hum some of them, such as *Nini la Chance* and *Cho ka ka o*.

When her adored husband Bruno died in the late 1980s, she retired from show business and took a well-earned rest. But not for long. In 1999 Annie, then 70 years old, was back on the boards at the side of her good friend Charles Aznavour. Still as bubbling with energy as she had been 50 years earlier.

At the same time this *vis comica* is seldom destructive. And conversely, critically-inclined artists who take themselves seriously do not necessarily have to suffer from affectation. Detachment stimulates a longing for exploration, which in literature has given occasion for a frequently occurring game with language – if only because, of course, the language in a bilingual country like Belgium can never be obvious. In Jean-Pierre Verheggen's poetry, each verse bubbles with language inventiveness. Or, at a more "eloquent" level, it is expressed in the very creative (and, agreed, very amusing) Captain Haddock's treasure chest of abusive vocabulary who, as the painter Pierre Alechinsky once remarked, shows a very great similarity with the curses and insults to be gleaned from the painter James Ensor's writings. In Flemish literature, language exploration has been a tradition since Guido Gazelle in the 19th century and Paul van Ostaijen in the early 20th century. But except that the word play and puns bear witness to the critical attitude of the writer towards his material, they also reveal a *homo ludens* – a person at play – stronger than himself. Because in Belgium, although the situation may often look hopeless, for its citizens and artists it is never serious. Certainly not serious enough to lose the liking for jest in the process.

The Good Life and the Inner Man

During their most recent tour of inspection, the renowned Guide Michelin inspectors handed out a total of some 80 "stars" to Belgian restaurants. Although 2000, expressed in the number of Michelin stars awarded, could only be considered an average year at most, it nevertheless remains a considerable number. It is, in comparison, about half as many again as the Michelin inspectors could raise in terms of appreciation for the culinary achievements of the Netherlands, a neighbouring country that, in fact, has more than half as many more inhabitants than Belgium.

The annual award of stars always attracts the attention of the general public, so that the mass media like to write exhaustively about it. Most newspapers and women's weeklies for that matter publish extensive information about food and restaurants and it is certainly not only the women's magazines which print recipes. However, prices in the praiseworthy establishments, whether or not they have been awarded any stars, (or forks or chef's hats) are as a rule not of a level where everyone would be able to eat with any degree of regularity.

It could make a country appear a little odd, where the masses take such delight in the fact that the wealthy can dine in that degree of style. Even more so that, thanks to the media, those masses also know the names of chefs and restaurant managers like Pierre Wynants, Frank Fol or Roger Souvereyns, while the chance is minimal of their ever being able to justify tasting these culinary masterpieces in situ. Let alone the mostly extremely expensive accompanying wines served, (which provide the restaurant keepers with their highest profit margins) which also need to be paid for.

196

Pierre Wynants,
chef at Comme Chez Soi

Gastronomy in Belgium

"Tell me what you eat and I will tell you what you are." Escoffier, to whom contemporary French cuisine owes everything, once said: "To describe a nation's cuisine is to paint a picture from which you can read the civilisation of that nation."'

Our polymorphic nation is rooted in its soil. In Belgium the cuisine reflects the landscape by means of its produce, and those who glorify that produce. The land borders a sea that feeds us: waterzooi (a kind of thick chicken or fish casserole), paling in't groen (eels in chervil sauce), tomates crevettes (tomatoes stuffed with shrimps) and the unique mussels and chips, praised in song by the chansonnier Brel. The hop shoots, germinating in the Pajottenland celebrated by Breughel, lead us to Brussels. They are our caviar, our truffles. Its monastic beers, chocolates and chicory place Belgium on the gastronomic map of the world. In the Ardennes there is ham. The juniper berry characterises the classical dishes of French cuisine. As a splendid cheese of world fame, Herve caresses the most sensitive olfactory organ. Fancy breads, stoemp (a hotchpotch), meatballs, tarts with crusts as thick as a lumberjack's finger: it is a privilege to eat here.

Our food is healthy, hearty, tasty and simple. It is like the little characters Georges Simenon required at his table. It is an everyday cuisine, which is faithful to its ingredients. A kitchen that dresses up for feast days. One that keeps close track of economic and social changes, of the rhythm of life, concerns about diet and the perfection of domestic appliances. A cuisine *open to foreign influences – whether over the centuries these have come from friends or conquerors. This cuisine has never faltered on its foundations. It is sincere and welcoming, greedy but not gluttonous, a source of true happiness, not a deadly sin. The great chefs have understood this well, so that La Reynière, the gastronomic critic of Le Monde, was able to write that "Belgian restaurants are often better than French ones"'*

Guy Lemaire

Head of Production, RTBF
French-language television channel

In fact, though, that interest is not completely odd. These stars are seen as international symbols of honour – the "Oscars" as has sometimes been claimed – for a national know-how concerning an activity which everyone can appreciate in concrete terms. As a result they provide a subject of collective pride which appeals to the imagination. But even though Belgians too are not insensitive to the snobbish and status-raising aspects of the restaurant visit, the interest in Michelin stars principally reflects a common fixation. Belgians have a thing about eating, to an extent that they have retained the mythological epithet "Burgundian" – and one they will readily admit fits like a glove. That could very well have something to do with a certain affinity for the art of living but it has mainly evolved from history, including recent history in which the Belgians have endured periods of hunger and shortages. The memory lingers on. Not only are wartime children still recognisable for always clearing their plate, they have impressed on their own children and grandchildren that throwing away food is a "sin", which not only involves wasting money but is almost evil, a morally reprehensible deed.

In the continuation of this historical memory lies the possible explanation for a conclusion that celebrities from the Mecca of haute cuisine, Paris, have often made with regard to the Belgian restaurant scene: that the gourmands outnumber the gourmets, that there are more gluttons than gastronomes. Indeed, the plate may admittedly be piled higher in Belgium, the sauce could be a soupçon heavier, the accompanying piece of meat turn out to be a trifle larger, chips might be consumed in a wide variety of combinations. The chip, by the way,

198

belongs in the basic food category because it combines two primary ingredients of the popular cuisine: potatoes and fat. The hungry Belgian can still depend on a *frietkot* or *frituur* until the wee hours, architectural monsters which demonstrate the beauty of ugliness on every village square.

Belgian cuisine shows many similarities to the French; more precisely the restaurant happening has developed directly from it, from the time when the chefs, made redundant by the aristocracy after the French Revolution, settled in Brussels. However, it does distinguish itself from it by suppressing its finesse, considered to be too extreme. The culinary minimalism of the destruction of haute cuisine, for example, no matter how fashionable, never enjoyed much appeal in Belgium. It was commonly called "food for people who do not enjoy eating".

The restraint with regard to culinary frivolities and titbits leads to Belgian cuisine sometimes being on the conservative, careful side: it does not seek to astound but likes to call itself "honest". Neither does it pretend to produce anything other than what it produces – namely food. Expressed in straightforward terms: it is a matter of decent everyday food. Its reliability is popularly expressed by underlining the fact that all the basic ingredients are fresh and, whenever possible, "natural" and simple. For preference these are selected and purchased at the crack of dawn by the head chef in the local market (not by a kitchen hand sent out with a shopping list).

Clever use of "unique" local ingredients like chicory, asparagus or mussels (which moreover mostly come from the Netherlands) and of specific recipes like *waterzooi* (fish stew) or the classic *biefstuk-friet* (steak and chips) – with mayonnaise – formed the basis for many Belgian chefs' success abroad. With them they developed their own niche with which they could even expand into small international chains, like the Belgo restaurants, Léon de Bruxelles and Le Pain Quotidien, with outlets in London, New York and even Paris.

The care and attention Belgians devote to food (and drink) leads to the vital physical functions of feeding and refreshing oneself never being a purely pragmatic occasion. The availability of food and drink is easily associated with merriment, so that its consumption quickly becomes the scene of shared pleasure, leading to conviviality and sociability. They became an expression of a liking for the good life, the small pleasures of existence. Because "what we have had, no-one can take away from us". Eating and drinking is preferably a collective activity. There is nothing Belgium lacks less than restaurants, cafés, taverns, brasseries, coffee houses, tea rooms and the like. They are less places where something is consumed than meeting places and social centres.

Of course, the circumstances need to be conducive. Interested in quality or not, the average present-day employee gets his daily mush from the works canteen or goes to fetch a sandwich from the snack bar around the corner from the office and in the evening slips a frozen meal into the microwave. Without doubt, young people like to be members of the faithful and

Famous and Memorable Belgians. These too are Belgians

enthusiastic clientele of the local outlet of American fast-food chains. Quick is Belgium's own chain of hamburger restaurants. And more exotic refinement is just as easy to find. Partly as a result of the immigration waves the "Italian" and the "Chinese" have started up in large numbers and Mediterranean cuisine has also found a permanent place for itself.

When it comes to drink, Belgium is primarily a beer country. The specialised café still has well over 100 different kinds of beer in stock, from the common lager to the heady Abbey beer, in a countless, sometimes highly imaginative variety of flavours, colours, aromas, alcohol levels – and names. Until well into the 20th century, practically every village had its own brewery. Their small scale made most of them unprofitable as time passed, resulting in the disappearance of many famous brands. Economic concentration led to most of the surviving brands of beer being housed with what has finally become known as Interbrew. Thanks to its large domestic market, of which it controls almost two-thirds, this company could develop into one of the major brewers in the world, with outlets in a many of countries. Apart from the Dutch Heineken, for example, (which Belgians do not recognise as "real" beer) it nevertheless does not market its own brand world-wide but principally commercialises local products, including the Canadian Labatt and the British Whitbread.

Proportionately, however, Belgians are not the greatest beer drinkers in the world. Per capita they are the greatest consumers of champagne and wine in the world, although

The Froth of Life

"Hello there ... what're you drinking?" In Belgium, the hearty welcome accorded to visitors involves a raised glass. A glass of beer is very normal here. Logical: even before Caesar had written that the Belgians were the bravest among all the Gauls, the tribes populating our territory were already very partial to beer. It is no coincidence that St Arnold, the patron saint of brewers, who as bishop of Soissons stemmed the tidal wave wrought by the plague by recommending beer instead of water, came into the world in Flanders. Nor any less a coincidence that behind the mythical figure of King Gambrinus, one can recognise the Duke of Brabant, John I (Primus), who was unmatched, both as a warrior and Epicurean, and left a permanent mark on 13th-century history. Since then the noble art of brewing has not only been passed on from generation to generation in the abbeys, but also in towns, where inspired artists and writers alike discovered that unleashing their creative energies proved thirsty work.

In 1900 there were more than 3,000 breweries in Belgium. As provider of employment, the brewer was an influential dignitary and often held the office of mayor. And if he was not the most senior magistrate in town he was, according to the poet Emile Verhaeren, its king.

Today there are little more than 100 brewers remaining. Although he no longer consumes 100 litres per year, the Belgian has remained faithful to his beer. And if there is a spot where Flemings, French and German-speakers are on the same wavelength, then it is in the bar. The bonhomie which prevails is equalled only by their devotion to the royal family and the performance of their sportsmen – if they win, at least. Time stands still at the bar, while comparing the distinctive characteristics of our hundreds of different types of beer! Not only the quantity but also the quality are discussed. Many of the beers are unique.

Of those beers brewed within abbey walls by Cistercian monks, there are only six on the planet permitted to carry the name Trappist. And all six of them are Belgian. There's a good language balance: three Walloon Trappists (Rochefort, Orval and Chimay) and three Flemish (Westvleteren, Westmalle and Achel). But Belgium is also the land of geuze (a sweetish, fruit-flavoured beer) and kriek (black cherry beer) - especially in Brussels and its surroundings - of the veritable Witte, of the red beers which have been christened the Flemish burgundies.

This diversity needs to be viewed in relation to the successive occupations to which our forefathers have been subjected. Good heavens! The Belgians have always fought tooth and nail to defend their individuality. Including their favourite drink! Today, Belgian beer is one of the cherries on our export cake. A few foreign brewers have even tried to emulate it ... but have never equalled it. So ...cheers, to your very good health!

Christian Laporte
Journalist with daily Le Soir

themselves they do not produce anything significant. To avoid any misunderstandings: this should not create the impression that Belgians suffer above average from obesity, heart and vascular disorders or alcoholism. After all, the art of living also assumes a kind of moderation.

If there are good historical reasons why Belgians do not like skimping on their food, the same applies to their sugar consumption. Sugar was traditionally a cheap source of energy and that became extended in a refined and by no means stingy production and consumption of confectionery and patisserie of all kinds. Certainly chocolate — in bars or artistically worked into the often sophisticated chocolates — endowed Belgium with a certain magic, also internationally, with makes like Côte d'Or, Galler, Godiva, Guylian, Callebaut and Leonidas. Or, as they are known throughout the United States, quite simply "Belgian chocolates".

Wittamer
© photo: Jean-Pierre Gabriel

Antwerp has its port, its diamonds, its zoo and its Rubens. But Antwerp also has its fashion. Antwerp couturiers have gained an international reputation as the absolute top. They turn up in fashion magazines and leading newspapers, and are placed firmly in the same rank with great established names such as Versace, Armani or Chanel.

This is how it happened: 20 years ago, in 1980-81, six designers graduated from the School of Fashion Design at Antwerp Academy of Fine Arts (now Antwerp College). They had talent, collaborated on commercial lines in the Belgian fashion trade and saved their money. Until in 1986 they presented their first collection in London. Each did their own thing, only they jointly hired a lorry to get there, almost their only real link, except for their talent and the will to make something of it. Their names were Dries Van Noten, Dirk Bikkembergs, Walter Van Beirendonck, Dirk Van Saene, Ann Demeulemeester and Marina Yee. Much too difficult, these names, for the English press, who called them the 'Antwerp Six'. Soon afterwards this same Antwerp Six went to Paris, again with their own collections, their own concepts. They were noticed

205

Dries Van Noten

and made a hit, so that they soon found it necessary to take part in the fashion round. But they continued doing this in their own way: obstinately and with conviction. There was also a seventh: Martin Margiela. He had graduated with the Six, but then moved to Paris to work for Jean-Paul Gaultier. As luck had it, in the late 1980s he too started to do his own thing and returned to his roots: the Antwerp school.

Today they have acquired international fame in their small world. Every season people look out for the shows of Dries Van Noten, Ann Demeulemeester, Dirk Bikkembergs, Dirk Van Saene, Martin Margiela and Walter Van Beirendonck (Marina Yee has not participated for some years, but is now reported to be working on a comeback). And their impact is great. Van Beirendonck dressed U2 and won the Flemish design prize, Martin Margiela has a contract as a designer with Hermes, the prestigious Paris fashion house, and so we could go on.

Fortunately it does not end with the Antwerp Six (or Seven). Another generation has now emerged, whose impact is if possible even greater. Véronique Branquinho, AF Vandevorst, Jurgi Persoons, Angelo Figus, Bernhard Willhelm and Patrick Van Ommeslaeghe also graduated from Antwerp.

They too ventured to design their own collection which they presented in Paris. And in their case too a bell began to ring with the public: new talent! Raf Simons did not study fashion, but industrial design, but he is also part of this second generation of couturiers from Antwerp. And he too features in the latest international fashion magazines. More: in the January issue of I-D, the British journal, Simons was 'guest editor'.

Is the younger generation different from the Six? No, they all display the same talent and enthusiasm; they all think conceptually and holistically. Though everyone knows that the path had already been smoothed for the second generation. Because it is still true today: Paris is keeping a very keen eye on what comes out of Belgium (no, Antwerp). But designers such as Xavier Delcour, Olivier Theyskens and Jose Enrique Ona Selfa, have also found the way to Paris. They too can count on applause there. Theyskens has even dressed Madonna. Only: they do not come from Antwerp but from Brussels. What a British journalist once said about the Six, therefore no longer applies: "What is it about Antwerp designers; can it be something in the water?"

Veerle Windels
Freelance fashion journalist

Olivier Strelli © Belga

Famous and Memorable Belgians. These too are Belgians